THE OLD WORLD
AND THE NEW
1492–1650

THE WILES LECTURES
GIVEN AT THE QUEEN'S UNIVERSITY
BELFAST
1969

J M Elliott
1975.

CAMBRIDGE STUDIES IN
EARLY MODERN HISTORY

Edited by
PROFESSOR J. H. ELLIOTT
King's College, University of London
and
PROFESSOR H. G. KOENIGSBERGER
Cornell University

The idea of an 'Early Modern' period of European history from the fifteenth to the late eighteenth century is now finding wide acceptance among historians. The purpose of Cambridge Studies in Early Modern History is to publish monographs and studies which will help to illuminate the character of the period as a whole, and in particular to focus attention on a dominant theme within it—the interplay of continuity (the continuity of medieval ideas, and forms of political and social organization) and change (the impact of new ideas, new methods and new demands on the traditional structures).

AMERICA

MAR DEL NORTE

TROPICO DE CANCER

EQVINOCIAL

TROPICO DE CAPRICORN

TERRA AVSTRALIS INCOGNITA

A la Espada . y el compas
Mas . y mas . y mas . y mas

THE
OLD WORLD
AND THE
NEW

1492-1650

by

J. H. ELLIOTT

Professor of History
King's College
University of London

CAMBRIDGE
AT THE UNIVERSITY PRESS
1972

Published by the Syndics of the Cambridge University Press
Bentley House, 200 Euston Road, London NW1 2DB
American Branch: 32 East 57th Street, New York, N.Y.10022

© Cambridge University Press 1970

Library of Congress Catalogue Card Number: 73–121362

ISBN
0 521 07937 3 clothbound
0 521 09621 9 paperback

First published 1970
Reprinted 1972

Printed in Great Britain by
Alden & Mowbray Ltd
at the Alden Press, Oxford

TO THE MEMORY OF
T.C.E.
1892–1969

CONTENTS

Frontispiece from Bernardo de Vargas Machuca, *Milicia y Descripción de las Indias* (Madrid, 1599).

PREFACE

The impact of the New World of America on sixteenth- and early seventeenth-century Europe is a large and ambitious theme, which should be discussed either in a very long book, or in a very short one. While I was pondering on it, I received the generous invitation of The Queen's University of Belfast to deliver the Wiles Lectures for 1969. One of the essential purposes of the Wiles Lectures is to encourage the discussion of broad issues which relate to the general history of civilization. The impact of the New World on the Old in the first century and a half after the discovery of America seemed eminently suited to this kind of treatment. This book, the text of my four lectures, is therefore very short.

The demands of time and space inevitably meant that my approach to the subject had to be highly selective. Some aspects had to be omitted, or could be only lightly touched upon; and I decided to concentrate almost exclusively on the Iberian world of central and southern America, at the expense of the Anglo-French world of the north. Although this is no doubt regrettable, my terminal date of 1650 makes the neglect of northern America less serious than it would have been if I had been examining the entire seventeenth century. While writing the lectures, I felt that the gain in unity and coherence of theme might go some way to compensate for the omission of much that would necessarily have been included in a large and comprehensive volume. The same consideration has guided my preparation of the lectures for publication. It seemed wiser to leave them very much in the form in which they were originally given, than to alter the general balance by expanding them into a book of conventional size.

One of the most attractive features of the Wiles Lectures is the special provision for the invitation to Belfast of a number of guests who join members of the academic staff of The Queen's University in the evening discussion which follows each lecture. The discussions on this occasion were both lively and interesting, and I have done my best to bear in mind the general tenor of our conversations

ix

Preface

when preparing the lectures for the press. I wish to record here my gratitude to the Astor, Leverhulme and Rockefeller Foundations for generous assistance towards travel and research in Latin America, which first opened my eyes to the historical possibilities to be found in the study of the relationship between the Old World and the New. I am grateful, too, to Mr Thomas R. Adams and the staff of the John Carter Brown Library in Providence, Rhode Island, for their kindness and help during all too brief an exploration of a collection which is brilliantly focused on the theme of this book. Above all, I am grateful to Mrs Janet Boyd and the Trustees of the Wiles Foundation for providing the inspiration and the excuse for this book, and to my friends and colleagues at The Queen's University of Belfast for ensuring that its trial run took place in the most pleasant and favourable conditions.

J. H. E.

King's College
London
December 1969

THE UNCERTAIN IMPACT

Nearly three hundred years after Columbus's first voyage of discovery, the Abbé Raynal, that eager inquirer after other men's truths, offered a prize for the essay which would best answer the following questions. Has the discovery of America been useful or harmful to mankind? If useful, how can its usefulness be enhanced? If harmful, how can the harm be diminished? Cornelius De Pauw had recently described the discovery of the New World as the most calamitous event in human history,[1] and Raynal was taking no chances. 'No event', he had cautiously begun his vast and laborious *Philosophical and Political History of the Settlements and Trade of the Europeans in the East and West Indies*, 'has been so interesting to mankind in general, and to the inhabitants of Europe in particular, as the discovery of the new world, and the passage to India by the Cape of Good Hope.'[2] It took the robust Scottish forthrightness of Adam Smith, whose view of the impact of the discoveries was generally favourable, to turn this non-committal passage into an *ex cathedra* historical pronouncement: 'the discovery of America, and that of a passage to the East Indies by the Cape of Good Hope, are the two greatest and most important events recorded in the history of mankind'.[3]

But in what, precisely, did their importance lie? As the candidates for Raynal's essay prize soon found out for themselves, this was by no means easy to decide. Of the eight essays which have survived, four took an optimistic view of the consequences of America's discovery, and dwelt at length on the resulting commercial advantages. But optimists and pessimists alike tended to wander uncertainly through three centuries of European history, anxiously

[1] Cornelius De Pauw, *Recherches Philosophiques sur les Américains*, in *Œuvres Philosophiques* (Paris, 1794), vol. i, p. ii. First published 1768.
[2] English translation (Dublin, 1776), i, 1. Original French version published in 1770.
[3] *The Wealth of Nations* (1776), ed. Edwin Cannan (reprinted University Paperbacks, London, 1961), ii, 141.

searching for pieces of stray ammunition with which to bombard their predetermined targets. In the end, it was perhaps not surprising that standards were considered insufficiently high, and no prize was awarded.[1]

Raynal's formulation of his questions no doubt tended to prompt philosophical speculation and dogmatic assertion, rather than rigorous historical inquiry. But this was less easily evaded in 1792, when the Académie Française asked competitors to examine the influence of America on the 'politics, commerce and customs of Europe'. It is difficult not to sympathize with the sentiments of the anonymous prize-winner. 'What a vast and inexhaustible subject', he sighed. 'The more one studies it, the more it grows.' Nevertheless, he succeeded in covering a great deal of ground in his eighty-six pages. As might have been expected, he was happier with America's political and economic influence on Europe than with its moral influence, which he regarded as pernicious. But he showed himself aware of the concealed danger in this enterprise—the danger of attributing all the major changes in modern European history to the discovery of America. He also made a genuine attempt, in language which may not sound totally unfamiliar to our own generation, to weigh up the profits and the losses of discovery and settlement. 'If those Europeans who devoted their lives to developing the resources of America had instead been employed in Europe in clearing forests, and building roads, bridges and canals, would not Europe have found in its own bosom the most important objects which it derives from the other world, or their equivalent? And what innumerable products would the soil of Europe not have yielded, if it had been brought to the degree of cultivation of which it is capable?'[2]

In a field where there are so many variables, and where the qualitative and the quantitative are so inextricably interwoven, even the modern arts of econometric history cannot do much to help us

[1] For Raynal's essay prize see Durand Echeverria, *Mirage in the West* (1957, reprinted Princeton, 1968), p. 173, which lists the titles of the surviving essays. See also A. Feugère, *L'Abbé Raynal* (Angoulême, 1922), pp. 343–6.

[2] *Discours composé en 1788, qui a remporté le prix sur la question : quelle a été l'influence de l'Amérique sur la politique, le commerce, et les mœurs de l'Europe?* (Paris, 1792), pp. 8 and 77–8.

assess the relative costs and benefits involved in the discovery and exploitation of America by Europe. Yet the impossibility of precise measurement should not be allowed to act as a deterrent to the study of a subject which has been regarded, at least since the late eighteenth century, as central to the history of Europe and the modern world.

For all the interest and importance of the theme, the historiography of the impact of America on Europe has enjoyed a distinctly chequered career. The eighteenth-century debate was conducted in terms which suggest that the participants were more concerned to confirm and defend their personal prejudices about the nature of man and society than to obtain a careful historical perspective on the contribution of the New World to Europe's economic and cultural development.[1] It was not until Humboldt published his *Cosmos* in 1845 that the reactions of the first Europeans, and especially of the Spaniards, to the alien environment of America assumed their proper place in a great geographical and historical synthesis, which made some attempt to consider what the revelation of the New World had meant to the Old.

Nineteenth-century historiography did not show any great interest in pursuing Humboldt's more original lines of inquiry. The discovery and settlement of the New World were incorporated into an essentially Europocentric conception of history, where they were depicted as part of that epic process by which the Renaissance European first became conscious of the world and of man, and then by degrees imposed his own dominion over the newly-discovered races of a newly-discovered world. In this particular story of European history—which was all too easily identified with universal history—there was a tendency to place the principal emphasis on the motives, methods and achievements of the explorers and conquerors. The impact of Europe on the world (which was regarded as a transforming, and ultimately beneficial, impact) seemed a subject of greater interest and concern than the impact of the world on Europe.

Twentieth-century European historiography has tended to pursue

[1] For the eighteenth-century debate see especially A. Gerbi, *La Disputa del Nuovo Mondo* (Milan, 1955; Spanish translation, *La Disputa del Nuevo Mundo*, Mexico, 1960).

a similar theme, although from a very different standpoint. The retreat of European imperialism has led to a reassessment—often very harsh—of the European legacy. At the same time the development of anthropology and archaeology has led to a reassessment— sometimes very favourable—of the pre-European past of former colonial societies. Where European historians once wrote with the confidence born of an innate sense of European superiority, they now write burdened with the consciousness of European guilt.

It is no accident that some of the most important historical work of our own age—preoccupied as it is with the problem of European and non-European, of black and white—should have been devoted to the study of the social, demographic and psychological consequences for non-European societies of Europe's overseas expansion. Perhaps future generations will detect in our concern with these themes some affinity between the historians of the eighteenth and twentieth centuries. For Raynal and his friends were similarly consumed by guilt and by doubt. Their hesitancy in evaluating the consequences of the discovery and conquest of America sprang precisely from the dilemma involved in attempting to reconcile the record of economic and technical progress since the end of the fifteenth century with the record of the sufferings endured by the defeated societies. The very extent of their preoccupation with the great moral issue of their own times, the issue of slavery, helped to create a situation not without its parallels today. For if their preoccupation stimulated them to ask historical questions, it also tempted them to reply with unhistorical answers.

The Académie Française competition of 1792 shows that one of those questions concerned the impact of overseas expansion on Europe itself; and it is not surprising to find a renewed interest in this same question today. As Europe again becomes acutely aware of the ambivalence of its relationship to the outer world, so it also becomes aware of the possibility of seeing itself in a different perspective—as part of a universal community of mankind whose existence has exercised its own subtle and transforming influences on the history of Europe. The awareness is salutary, although it contains an element of narcissism, to which the eighteenth century self-indulgently succumbed. Moreover, where the relationship with

America is concerned, this element is likely to be particularly well represented. For this has always been a *special* relationship, in the sense that America was peculiarly the artefact of Europe, as Asia and Africa were not. America and Europe were for ever inseparable, their destinies interlocked.

The part played by the American myth in the spiritual and intellectual development of Europe has now become a commonplace of historical study. In the early years of this century, the impressive work of Gabriel Chinard on America and the exotic dream in French literature[1] revealed in brilliant detail the fluctuating process by which an idealized New World helped to sustain the hopes and aspirations of the Old until the moment when Europe was ready to accept and act upon America's message of renovation and revolution. Chinard's work was complemented and amplified by Geoffrey Atkinson's study of French geographical literature and ideas,[2] and, more recently, by Antonello Gerbi's massive survey of the eighteenth-century debate on America as a corrupt or an innocent world.[3] One further book stands out amidst the rapidly growing literature on Europe and the American dream—*The Invention of America*, by the distinguished Mexican philosophical historian, Edmundo O'Gorman, who has ingeniously argued that America was not discovered but invented by sixteenth-century Europeans.[4]

Alongside these contributions to the study of the myth of America in European thought, an increasing amount of attention has been devoted, especially in the Hispanic world, to the writings of the Spanish chroniclers, missionaries and officials, as interpreters of the American scene. A vast amount of close textual study still remains to be undertaken, but enough has already been achieved to confirm the justice of Humboldt's slightly condescending verdict: 'If we carefully examine the original works of the earliest historians of the Conquista, we are astonished at finding in a Spanish author of the sixteenth century, the germs of so many important physical

[1] *L'Exotisme Américain dans la Littérature Française au XVIe Siècle* (Paris, 1911) and *L'Amérique et le Rêve Exotique dans la Littérature Française au XVIIe et au XVIIIe Siècle* (Paris, 1913).
[2] *Les Nouveaux Horizons de la Renaissance Française* (Paris, 1935).
[3] See above, p. 3, note 1.
[4] (Bloomington, 1961).

truths.'[1] There are still great opportunities for research into the Spanish texts, as indeed into the general sixteenth-century literature of exploration and discovery. But the most rewarding results of this textual research are likely to come from intelligent attempts to set it into a wider context of information and ideas. The evidence of the texts can tell us much that we still need to know about non-European societies, by providing the essential material for 'ethnohistory', which sets the results of ethnographic study against European historical records. It can also tell us something of interest about European society—about the ideas, attitudes and preconceptions which made up the mental baggage of Early Modern Europeans on their travels through the world. What did they see or fail to see? Why did they react as they did? It is the attempt to suggest answers to some of these questions which makes Margaret Hodgen's recent history of *Early Anthropology in the Sixteenth and Seventeenth Centuries*[2] such an important pioneering work.

This select company of books stands out, not only because of their intrinsic excellence, but also because of the particular line of approach adopted by their authors. All of them have sought, in some way, to relate the European response to the non-European world to the general history of European civilization and ideas. It is here that the most promising opportunities are to be found; and here, too, that there is most need for some kind of reassessment and synthesis. For the literature on the discovery and colonization of the New World is now enormous, but it is also in many respects fragmentary and disconnected, as if it formed a special field of historical study on its own.

'What is lacking in English is an attempt to tie in exploration with European history as a whole.'[3] This lack provides some justification for an attempt to synthesize, in brief compass, the present state of thought about the impact made by the discovery and settlement of America on Early Modern Europe. Any such attempt must clearly lead into several different fields of inquiry, for America impinged on sixteenth- and early seventeenth-century Europe at innumerable points. Its discovery had important *intellectual*

---

[1] *Cosmos* (vol. ii, London, 1848), p. 295.   [2] (Philadelphia, 1964).
[3] J. R. Hale, *Renaissance Exploration* (BBC Publications, London, 1968), p. 104.

consequences, in that it brought Europeans into contact with new lands and peoples, and in so doing challenged a number of traditional European assumptions about geography, theology, history and the nature of man. America also constituted an *economic* challenge for Europe, in that it proved to be at once a source of supply for produce and for objects for which there existed a European demand, and a promising field for the extension of European business enterprise. Finally, the acquisition by European states of lands and resources in America was bound to have important *political* repercussions, in that it affected their mutual relations by bringing about changes in the balance of power.

Any examination of European history in the light of an external influence upon it, carries with it the temptation to find traces of this influence everywhere. But the absence of influence is often at least as revealing as its presence; and if some fields of thought are still curiously untouched by the experience of America, a hundred years or more after its discovery, this too can tell us something about the character of European civilization. From 1492 the New World was always present in European history, although its presence made itself felt in different ways at different times. It is for this reason that America and Europe should not be subjected to a historiographical divorce, however shadowy their partnership may often appear before the later seventeenth century. Properly, their histories should constitute a continuous interplay of two distinctive themes.

One theme is represented by the attempt of Europe to impose its own image, its own aspirations, and its own values, on a newly-discovered world, together with the consequences for that world of its actions. The other treats of the way in which a growing awareness of the character, the opportunities and the challenges represented by the New World of America helped to shape and transform an Old World which was itself striving to shape and transform the New. The first of these themes has traditionally received more emphasis than the second, although, ultimately, the two are equally important and should remain inseparable. But at this moment the second is in need of more historical attention than the first. From around 1650 the histories of Europe and America have been reasonably well integrated. But for the sixteenth and early seventeenth centuries, the significance of America for Europe still awaits a full assessment.

'It is a striking fact', wrote the Parisian lawyer, Etienne Pasquier, in the early 1560s, 'that our classical authors had no knowledge of all this America, which we call New Lands.'[1] With these words he caught something of the importance of America for the Europe of his day. Here was a totally new phenomenon, quite outside the range of Europe's accumulated experience and of its normal expectation. Europeans knew something, however vaguely and inaccurately, about Africa and Asia. But about America and its inhabitants they knew nothing. It was this which differentiated the response of sixteenth-century Europeans to America from that of the fifteenth-century Portuguese to Africa. The nature of the Africans was known, at least in a general way. That of the Americans was not. The very fact of America's existence, and of its gradual revelation as an entity in its own right, rather than as an extension of Asia, constituted a challenge to a whole body of traditional assumptions, beliefs and attitudes. The sheer immensity of this challenge goes a long way towards explaining one of the most striking features of sixteenth-century intellectual history—the apparent slowness of Europe in making the mental adjustments required to incorporate America within its field of vision.

At first sight, the evidence for the existence of a time-lag between the discovery of America and Europe's assimilation of that discovery does not seem entirely clear cut. There is, after all, ample evidence of the excitement provoked in Europe by the news of Columbus's landfall. 'Raise your spirits ... Hear about the new discovery!' wrote the Italian humanist Peter Martyr to the count of Tendilla and the archbishop of Granada on 13 September 1493. Christopher Columbus, he reported, 'has returned safe and sound. He says that he has found marvellous things, and he has produced gold as proof of the existence of mines in those regions.' And Martyr then went on to recount how Columbus had found men who went around naked, and lived content with what nature gave them. They had kings; they fought among each other with staves and bows and arrows; although they were naked, they competed for power, and they married. They

---

[1] *Les Œuvres d'Estienne Pasquier*, vol. ii (Amsterdam, 1723), bk. iii, letter iii, p. 55.

worshipped the celestial bodies, but the exact nature of their religious beliefs was still unknown.[1]

That Martyr's excitement was widely shared is indicated by the fact that Columbus's first letter was printed and published nine times in 1493 and had reached some twenty editions by 1500.[2] The frequent printing of this letter and of the reports of later explorers and *conquistadores*; the fifteen editions of Francanzano Montalboddo's collection of voyages, the *Paesi Novamente Retrovati*, first published at Venice in 1507; the great mid-century compilation of voyages by Ramusio—all this testifies to the great curiosity and interest aroused in sixteenth-century Europe by the news of the discoveries.[3]

Similarly, it is not difficult to find resounding affirmations by individual sixteenth-century writers of the magnitude and significance of the events which were unfolding before their eyes. Guicciardini lavished praise on the Spaniards and Portuguese, and especially on Columbus, for the skill and courage 'which has brought to our age the news of such great and unexpected things'.[4] Juan Luis Vives, who was born in the year of America's discovery, wrote in 1531 in the dedication of his *De Disciplinis* to John III of Portugal: 'truly, the globe has been opened up to the human race'.[5] Eight years later, in 1539, the Paduan philosopher Lazzaro Buonamico introduced a theme which would be elaborated upon in the 1570s by the French writer Louis Le Roy, and would become a commonplace of European historiography: 'Do not believe that there exists anything more

---

[1] *Epistolario de Pedro Mártir de Anglería*, ed. José López de Toro (Documentos Inéditos para la Historia de España, vols. ix-xii, Madrid, 1953-7), vol. ix, letter 133, p. 242.
[2] For the diffusion of news about Columbus's first voyage, see S. E. Morison, *Christopher Columbus, Mariner* (London, 1956), p. 108; Charles Verlinden and Florentino Pérez-Embid, *Cristóbal Colón y el Descubrimiento de América* (Madrid, 1967), pp. 91-4; Howard Mumford Jones, *O Strange New World* (New York, 1964), pp. 1-2.
[3] For Montalboddo and Ramusio, see D. B. Quinn, 'Exploration and the Expansion of Europe' in vol. i of the *Rapports* of the XIIth International Congress of Historical Sciences (Vienna, 1965), pp. 45-59, and G. B. Parks, *The Contents and Sources of Ramusio's Navigationi* (New York, 1955). Interesting discussions of the diffusion of news about the discoveries are to be found in *Les Aspects Internationaux de la Découverte Océanique aux XVe et XVIe Siècles* (Actes du Cinquième Colloque International d'Histoire Maritime), ed. M. Mollat and P. Adam (Paris, 1966).
[4] *Storia d'Italia*, ed. C. Panigada (Bari, 1929), ii, 131 (Bk. vi, c. ix).
[5] I am indebted for this and other references to America in the works of Vives to Dr Abdón Salazar of the Department of Spanish, King's College, London.

honourable to our or the preceeding age than the invention of the printing press and the discovery of the new world; two things which I always thought could be compared, not only to Antiquity, but to immortality.'[1] And in 1552 Gómara, in the dedication to Charles V of his *General History of the Indies*, wrote perhaps the most famous, and certainly the most succinct, of all assessments of the significance of 1492: 'The greatest event since the creation of the world (excluding the incarnation and death of Him who created it) is the discovery of the Indies.'[2]

Yet against these signs of awareness must be set the no less striking signs of unawareness of the importance both of the discovery of America and of its discoverer. The historical reputation of Columbus is a subject which has not yet received all the attention it deserves;[3] but the treatment of Columbus by sixteenth-century writers indicates something of the difficulty which they encountered in seeing his achievement in any sort of historical perspective. With one or two exceptions they showed little interest in his personality and career, and some of them could not even get his Christian name right. When he died in Valladolid, the city chronicle failed to record the fact.[4] It seemed as though Columbus might be doomed to oblivion, partly perhaps because he failed to conform to the sixteenth-century canon of the hero-figure, and partly because the true significance of his achievement was itself so hard to grasp.

There were, however, always a few spirits, particularly in his native Italy, who were prepared to give Columbus his due. The determination of his son, Hernando, to perpetuate his memory, and the publication in Venice in 1571 of the famous biography,[5] helped

---

[1] Cited by Elisabeth Feist Hirsch, *Damião de Gois* (The Hague, 1967), p. 103. See also Louis Le Roy, *De la Vicissitude ou Variété des Choses en l'Univers* (3rd ed. Paris, 1579), fs. 98–99 v.

[2] Francisco López de Gómara, *Primera Parte de la Historia General de las Indias* (Biblioteca de Autores Españoles, vol. 22, Madrid, 1852), p. 156.

[3] But see the valuable pioneering essay by Leicester Bradner, 'Columbus in Sixteenth-Century Poetry', in *Essays Honoring Lawrence C. Wroth* (Portland, Maine, 1951), pp. 15–30.

[4] Cesare de Lollis, *Cristoforo Colombo nella Leggenda e nella Storia* (3rd ed. Rome, 1923), p. 313.

[5] *Vida del Almirante Don Cristóbal Colón*, ed. Ramon Iglesia (Mexico, 1947). The traditional attribution of the biography to Hernando Colón is rejected by Alexandre Cioranescu in 'Christophe Colomb: Les Sources de sa Biographie', in the volume of

to keep his name before the world. When Sir Francis Bacon included a statue of Columbus in the gallery in New Atlantis devoted to the statues of 'all principal inventors', his intended tribute to the discoverer of America was not in fact very original. In his *History of the New World,* published in 1565, the Italian Benzoni alleged that if Columbus had 'lived in the time of the Greeks or of the Romans, or of any other liberal nation, they would have erected a statue'. The same idea was expressed a few years earlier by another of Columbus's compatriots, Ramusio, who in turn probably lifted it from the *History of the Indies,* written by his Spanish friend, Gonzalo Fernández de Oviedo. Recalling famous statues of classical antiquity, Oviedo insisted that Columbus, 'the first discoverer and finder of these Indies', was even more worthy of commemoration. 'As a brave and wise sailor, and a courageous captain, he showed to us this New World, which is so full of gold that thousands of such statues could have been made out of the gold that is sent to Spain. But he is still more worthy of fame and glory for having brought the Catholic faith to these parts . . . '[1]

Gold and conversion—these were the two most immediate and obvious connotations of America, and those most likely to be associated with the name of its discoverer. It was only by slow degrees that Columbus began to acquire the status of a hero. He figured as the central protagonist in a number of Italian epic poems written in the last two decades of the sixteenth century, and in 1614 he at last appeared as the hero of a Spanish drama, with the publication of Lope de Vega's extraordinary play, *El Nuevo Mundo descubierto por Cristóbal Colón.* Lope shows a genuine historical appreciation of the significance of Columbus's achievement when he puts into the mouth of Ferdinand the Catholic a speech affirming the traditional cosmography of a tripartite globe, and scoffing at the possibility that there might exist a portion of the world still to be discovered. At the

---

proceedings of the tenth international conference of Etudes Humanistes held at Tours in 1966, and published under the title of *La Découverte de l'Amérique* (Paris, 1968).

[1] *The Works of Francis Bacon,* ed. J. Spedding, iii (London, 1857), 165–6; Girolamo Benzoni, *History of the New World* (Hakluyt Society, 1st Series, vol. 21, London, 1857), p. 35; G. B. Ramusio, *Terzo Volume delle Navigationi et Viaggi* (Venice, 1556), f. 5; Gonzalo Fernández de Oviedo, *Historia General y Natural de las Indias* (Biblioteca de Autores Españoles, vols. 117–21, Madrid, 1959), i, 167.

same time, his Columbus, as a dreamer mocked by the world, has already started on his career as the romantic hero who becomes the symbol of man's unquenchable spirit of discovery.

There were already intimations of this romanticization of Columbus during the sixteenth century. But more commonly he was set within the framework of a providential interpretation of history, which depicted him as a divinely appointed instrument for the spreading of the gospel—and even here he was likely to find himself relegated to second place by the more obviously heroic figure of Hernán Cortés. But not even the mass-conversion of hitherto unknown peoples was sufficient of itself to ensure a firm place for Columbus, or Cortés, or for the New World, in the European consciousness. In some circles—especially certain humanist and religious circles, and in the merchant communities of some of Europe's leading cities—the interest was intense, although partial, and often specialized, in character. But it seems that the European reading public displayed no overwhelming interest in the newly-discovered world of America.

The evidence for this assertion unfortunately lacks the firm statistical foundation which it should properly possess. At present, the most comprehensive information about sixteenth-century reading tastes comes from France, where Atkinson's survey of geographical literature indicates that between 1480 and 1609 four times as many books were devoted to the Turks and Asia as to America, and that the proportion of books on Asia actually increased in the final decade of his chosen period.[1] For other parts of Europe, conclusions remain impressionistic. In England, there is little sign of literary interest before the 1550s, when the new Anglo-Spanish connection provided a belated stimulus. In Italy, the very considerable interest during the opening phase of the discoveries does not appear to have been maintained beyond the ending of active Italian participation around 1520; but a spate of translations of foreign accounts suggests that it revived sharply after 1550. Except for those with a professional interest in the subject, Spanish authors in the century following the discovery were strangely reticent about the New World. Until the publication in 1569 of the first part of Ercilla's *Araucana*, epic poems

[1] *Les Nouveaux Horizons*, pp. 10–12.

12

recounted the feats of Spanish arms in Italy and Africa, but ignored—
to the chagrin of Bernal Díaz—the no less heroic feats of Spanish
arms in the Indies. This neglect, in the nation where it is least to be
expected, is not easily explained. It may be that neither *conquistadores*
of relatively humble origins, nor their barbarian opponents, measured
up to the high standards required of epic heroes.[1]

But even if more statistical studies existed, it would not be easy to
interpret their conclusions. This is a field in which the attempt to
draw qualitative conclusions from quantitative data is more than
usually dangerous. A recent investigation has uncovered at least
sixty references to America in thirty-nine Polish books and manuscripts of the sixteenth and seventeenth centuries. The number is
not unimpressive, but on closer inspection it transpires that the
New World constantly reappears in a limited number of contexts—
either as a symbol of the exotic, or as a testimonial to the achievements of the church triumphant—and that sixteenth-century Poles
were not much interested in America.[2] Conversely, it could be
argued that the *qualitative* changes introduced into European
thought by accounts of the New World and its peoples, far outweigh
the quantity of information at the disposal of the reader. Montaigne
was dependent on Gómara's *History of the Indies* for much of his
information; but his reading of this one book, in the 1584 edition of
the French translation, had profound consequences for his whole
approach to the question of conquest and colonization.[3]

In spite of this, it is difficult not to be impressed by the strange
lacunae and the resounding silences in many places where references
to the New World could reasonably be expected. How are we to

1 For the literature of discovery in general, see Boies Penrose, *Travel and Discovery in
the Renaissance, 1420–1620* (Cambridge, Mass., 1960), c. 17 and bibliography. For the
impact on literature in England, R. R. Cawley, *Unpathed Waters: studies in the in-
fluence of voyages on Elizabethan Literature* (Oxford, 1940), and A. L. Rowse, *The
Elizabethans and America* (London, 1959), c. viii. For Italy, Rosario Romeo, *Le
Scoperte Americane nella Coscienza Italiana del Cinquecento* (Milan–Naples, 1954). For
Spain, Valentín de Pedro, *América en las Letras Españolas del Siglo de Oro* (Buenos
Aires, 1954), and Marcos A. Morínigo, *América en el Teatro de Lope de Vega* (Buenos
Aires, 1946).
2 Janusz Tazbir, 'La Conquête de l'Amérique à la Lumière de l'Opinion Polonaise',
Acta Poloniae Historica, xvii (1968), 5–22.
3 Pierre Villey, *Les Livres d'Histoire Moderne Utilisés par Montaigne* (Paris, 1908), p. 77,
and Gilbert Chinard, *L'Exotisme Américain*, c. ix.

explain the absence of any mention of the New World in so many memoirs and chronicles, including the memoirs of Charles V himself? How are we to explain the continuing determination, right up to the last two or three decades of the sixteenth century, to describe the world as if it were still the world as known to Strabo, Ptolemy and Pomponius Mela? How are we to explain the persistent reprinting by publishers, and the continuing use by schools, of classical cosmographies which were known to be outdated by the discoveries?[1] How are we to explain that a man as widely read and as curious as Bodin should have made so little use of the considerable information available to him about the peoples of the New World in the writing of his political and social philosophy?

The reluctance of cosmographers or of social philosophers to incorporate into their work the new information made available to them by the discovery of America provides an example of the wider problem arising from the revelation of the New World to the Old. Whether it is a question of the geography of America, its flora and fauna, or the nature of its inhabitants, the same kind of pattern seems constantly to recur in the European response. It is as if, at a certain point, the mental shutters come down; as if, with so much to see and absorb and understand, the effort suddenly becomes too much for them, and Europeans retreat to the half-light of their traditional mental world.

There is nothing very novel about the form of this sixteenth-century response. Medieval Europe had found it supremely difficult to comprehend and come to terms with the phenomenon of Islam; and the story of the attempt at understanding is an intricate story of the interplay of prejudice, puzzlement and indifference, where there is no clear linear progression, but rather a series of advances and retreats.[2] Nor is this a matter for surprise, for the attempt of one society to comprehend another inevitably forces it to reappraise

---

[1] For Renaissance geography in general, see François de Dainville, *La Géographie des Humanistes* (Paris, 1940). A fascinating example of the absence of interest in the New World in the geographical teaching provided in early sixteenth-century Nuremburg is provided by E. P. Goldschmidt, 'Not in Harrisse' in *Essays Honoring Lawrence C. Wroth*, pp. 129–41.

[2] See R. W. Southern, *Western Views of Islam in the Middle Ages* (Cambridge, Mass., 1962).

itself. In his essay on 'Understanding a Primitive Society', Professor Peter Winch writes: 'Seriously to study another way of life is necessarily to seek to extend our own—not simply to bring the other way within the already existing boundaries of our own, because the point about the latter in their present form, is that they *ex hypothesi* exclude that other.'[1] This process is bound to be an agonizing one, involving the jettisoning of many traditional preconceptions and inherited ideas. It is hardly surprising, then, if sixteenth-century Europeans either ignored the challenge or baulked at the attempt. There was, after all, an easier way out, neatly epitomized in 1528 by the Spanish humanist, Hernán Pérez de Oliva, when he wrote that Columbus set out on his second voyage 'to unite the world and give to those strange lands the form of our own'.[2]

'Give to those strange lands the form of our own.' Here, surely, is revealed that innate sense of superiority which has always been the worst enemy of understanding. How can we expect a Europe so conscious of its own infallibility—of its unique status and position in God's providential design—even to make the effort to come to terms with a world other than its own? But this Europe was not the closed Europe of an 'age of ignorance'.[3] Instead, it was Renaissance Europe—the Europe of 'the discovery of the world and of man'. If Renaissance ideas and attitudes played an important part—however elusive it may be to determine exactly *what* part—in prompting Europeans to set out on voyages of discovery and to extend their mental as well as their geographical horizons, might we not expect a new kind of readiness to respond to fresh information and fresh stimuli from a newly-discovered world?[4]

The conclusion does not necessarily follow. In some respects the Renaissance involved, at least in its earlier stages, a closing rather than an opening of the mind. The veneration of antiquity became more slavish; authority staked fresh claims against experience. Both the boundaries and the content of traditional disciplines such as cosmography or social philosophy had been clearly determined by

[1] In D. Z. Phillips, *Religion and Understanding* (Oxford, 1967), p. 30.
[2] *Historia de la Invención de las Yndias* (Bogotá, 1965), pp. 53–4.
[3] The phrase is that of R. W. Southern, *Western Views of Islam*, c. 1.
[4] This point is discussed by John Hale, 'A World Elsewhere' in *The Age of the Renaissance*, ed. Denys Hay (London, 1967), p. 339.

reference to the texts of classical antiquity, which acquired an extra degree of definitiveness when for the first time they were fixed on the printed page. Fresh information from alien sources was therefore liable to seem at worst incredible, at best irrelevant, when set against the accumulated knowledge of the centuries. Given this deference to authority, there was unlikely to be any undue precipitation, least of all in academic circles, to accept the New World into consciousness.

It is also possible that a society which is wrestling—as late medieval Christendom was wrestling—with great spiritual, intellectual and political problems, is too preoccupied with its internal upheavals to devote more than fitful attention to phenomena located on the periphery of its interests. It may be too much to expect such a society to make a further radical adjustment—and one which this time involves the assimilation of an entirely new range of alien experiences. Against this, however, it could be argued that a society which is in movement, and displays symptoms of dissatisfaction, is more likely to show itself capable of absorbing new impressions and experiences than a static society, satisfied with itself, and secure in the assurance of its own superiority.[1]

The degree of success or failure in sixteenth-century Europe's response to the Indies can to some extent be measured by reference to another response in a not dissimilar situation—the response of the Chinese of the T'ang dynasty to the reconquered tropical southern lands of Nam-Viet, which has recently been examined by Professor Edward Schafer, in his remarkable book, *The Vermilion Bird*.[2] His findings suggest that the difficulties confronting colonial officials of seventh-century China and of sixteenth-century Spain in assessing and describing an alien environment were by no means dissimilar, and that the nature of their response was much the same. The Chinese, like the Spaniards, observed and assiduously wrote down their observations, but they were, in Professor Schafer's words, the

---

[1] I am grateful to Dr Peter Burke of the University of Sussex for pointing out to me the contrasting examples of receptivity and resistance to change among the Ibo and the Pakot tribes, as described in W. R. Bascom and M. J. Herskovits, *Continuity and Change in African Cultures* (Chicago, 1959).

[2] (Berkeley, 1967). I am grateful to Professor J. H. Plumb for bringing this book to my notice.

'prisoners of their ecological lexicons'.[1] Their minds and imaginations were preconditioned, so that they saw what they expected to see, and ignored or rejected those features of life in the southern lands for which they were mentally unprepared. They found (because they expected to find) the inhabitants barbarian and apelike, and the tropical landscape unalluring. No doubt the tendency to think in clichés is the eternal hallmark of the official mind; but it was only slowly that the unfamiliar environment widened the perceptions of some of the Chinese in the southern lands, and enriched their literature and thought.

There was no European equivalent to the poetically evocative response of the Chinese to their strange new world, but America ultimately extended Europe's mental horizons in other, and perhaps more important, ways. In both instances, however, there was the same initial uncertainty, and the same slowness to respond. Given the great mental adjustments to be made, the response of sixteenth-century Europe was perhaps, after all, not as slow as it sometimes appears to be. Nor was it by any means as slow as might have been anticipated from Christendom's record during the preceding millennium. Early Modern Europe showed itself quicker to respond to the experience of the New World of America, than Medieval Europe to the experience of the world of Islam. This may suggest that the lessons taught by the Indies were more easily learnt, or that Europe at this moment was more ready to go to school. Probably it was a combination of both. No doubt it is possible to feel impatience at the slowness of the educational process—at the hesitations and the setbacks, and at the blind spots which still existed when the lessons were learnt. But there is also something rather moving about the groping of those sixteenth-century Europeans who sought to come to terms with the lands and peoples that had been so unexpectedly revealed to them on the far side of the Atlantic.

For the obstacles to the incorporation of the New World within Europe's intellectual horizon were formidable. There were obstacles of time and space, of inheritance, environment and language; and efforts would be required at many different levels before they were removed. At least four different processes were involved, each of

[1] P. 42.

which raised peculiar difficulties of its own. First of all there was the process of observation, as defined by Humboldt when he wrote: 'To see . . . is not to observe; that is, to compare and classify.'[1] The second process was description—depicting the unfamiliar in such a way that it could be grasped by those who had not seen it. The third was dissemination—the diffusion of new information, new images and new ideas, so that they became part of the accepted stock of mental furniture. And the fourth was comprehension—the ability to come to terms with the unexpected and the unfamiliar, to see them as phenomena existing in their own right, and (hardest of all) to shift the accepted boundaries of thought in order to include them.

If one asks *what* Europeans saw on arriving on the far side of the Atlantic, and *how* they saw it, much will inevitably depend on the kind of Europeans involved. The range of vision is bound to be affected both by background, and by professional interests. Soldiers, clerics, merchants, and officials trained in the law—these are the classes of men on whom we are dependent for most of our first-hand observation of the New World and its inhabitants. Each class had its own bias and its own limitations; and it would be interesting to have a systematic survey of the extent and nature of the bias for each professional group, and of the way in which it was mitigated or altered, in individual cases, by a humanist education.

One Spanish official in the Indies who transcended many of the limitations of his class, and achieved an unusual degree of insight into Quechua society by dint of learning the language, was Juan de Betanzos. In the dedication to his History of the Incas, written in 1551, he spoke of the difficulties he had met in composing the work. There was such a quantity of conflicting information, and he was concerned to find 'how differently the *conquistadores* speak about these things, and how far removed they are from Indian practice. And this I believe to be due to the fact that at that time they were not so much concerned with finding things out as with subjecting and acquiring the land. It was also because, coming new to the Indians, they did not know how to ask questions and find things out, for they lacked knowledge of the language; while the Indians,

[1] *Cosmos*, ii, 311.

18

for their part, were too frightened to give them a full account.'[1]

The professional preoccupations of the *conquistadores*, and the difficulties of conducting any form of effective dialogue with the Indians, are more than enough to account for the deficiencies of their reports as descriptions of the New World and its inhabitants; and it is a piece of unusual good fortune that the conquest of Mexico should have thrown up two soldier-chroniclers as shrewd in their observation and as vivid in their powers of description as Cortés and Bernal Díaz. In Cortés's letters of relation it is possible to see at work the process of observation, in Humboldt's sense of the word, as he attempts to bring the exotic into the range of the familiar by writing of Aztec temples as mosques, or by comparing the market-place of Tenochtitlán with that of Salamanca.[2] But there are obvious limits to Cortés's capacity as an observer, particularly when it comes to depicting the extraordinary landscape through which his invading army marched.

This failure to describe and communicate the physical characteristics of the New World is not peculiar to Cortés. Admittedly, the failure is by no means complete. The Italian Verrazano conveys a clear impression of the thickly forested character of the North American coast;[3] the French Calvinist minister, Jean de Léry, vividly describes the exotic flora and fauna of Brazil;[4] the Englishman, Arthur Barlowe, conjures up the sights and smells of the trees and flowers on the first Roanoke voyage.[5] Columbus himself shows at times a remarkable gift for realistic observation, although at other times the idealized landscape of the European imagination interposes itself between him and the American scene.[6] But so often the physical appearance of the New World is either totally ignored or

[1] *Crónicas Peruanas de Interés Indígena*, ed. F. Esteve Barba (Biblioteca de Autores Españoles, vol. 209, Madrid, 1968), 7.

[2] Hernán Cortés, *Cartas y Documentos*, ed. Mario Hernández Sánchez-Barba (Mexico, 1963), pp. 73 and 166.

[3] Voyage of 1524, in *Les Français en Amérique pendant la Première Moitié du XVIe Siècle*, ed. C. A. Julien, R. Herval, T. Beauchesne (Paris, 1946), pp. 51–76.

[4] *Histoire d'un Voyage fait en la Terre du Bresil* (La Rochelle, 1578), pp. 170 ff.

[5] *The Roanoke Voyages, 1584–1590*, ed. D. B. Quinn (Hakluyt Society, 2nd series, vols. 104–5, London, 1955), i, 94–5.

[6] See especially L. Olschki, 'What Columbus Saw on Landing in the West Indies', *Proceedings of the American Philosophical Society*, 84 (1941), 633–59.

else described in the flattest and most conventional phraseology. This off-hand treatment of nature contrasts strikingly with the many precise and acute descriptions of the native inhabitants. It is as if the American landscape is seen as no more than a backcloth against which the strange and perennially fascinating peoples of the New World are dutifully grouped.

This apparent deficiency in naturalistic observation may reflect a lack of interest among sixteenth-century Europeans, and especially those of the Mediterranean world, in landscape and in nature. It may reflect, too, the strength of traditional literary conventions. The Spanish soldier of fortune, Alonso Enríquez de Guzmán, who embarked for the New World in 1534, firmly announces in his autobiography: 'I will not tell you so much about what I saw as about what happened to me, because . . . this book is simply a book of my experiences.'[1] Unfortunately he proves as good as his word.

Even where Europeans in the New World had the desire to look, and the eyes to see, there is no guarantee that the image which presented itself to them—whether of peoples or of places—necessarily accorded with the reality. Tradition, experience and expectation were the determinants of vision. Even a presumably sober official of the Spanish Crown, Alonso de Zuazo, manages to transmute Hispaniola in 1518 into an enchanted island where the fountains play and the streams are lined with gold, and where nature yields her fruits in marvellous abundance.[2] Bernal Díaz, in many ways so down-to-earth and perceptive an observer, still looks at the conquest of Mexico through the haze of romances of chivalry. Verrazano brilliantly describes the Rhode Island Indians, with their dark hair, their bronzed colouring, their black and lively eyes. But were their faces really as 'gentle and noble as those of classical sculptures',[3] or was this the reaction of a man with a Florentine humanist upbringing, who had already created for himself a mental

---

[1] *Libro de la Vida y Costumbres de Don Alonso Enríquez de Guzmán*, ed. Hayward Keniston (Biblioteca de Autores Españoles, vol. 126, Madrid, 1960), p. 137.
[2] Cited by M. Jiménez de la Espada, *Relaciones Geográficas de Indias. Perú* (2nd ed., Biblioteca de Autores Españoles, vols. 183–5, Madrid, 1965), i, 11.
[3] *Les Français en Amérique*, ed. Julien, p. 64. For Verrazano's background and education see J. Habert, 'Jean de Verrazane: état de la question', *La Découverte de l'Amérique*. pp. 51–9.

image of the New World inspired by the Golden Age of antiquity?

It is hard to escape the impression that sixteenth-century Europeans, like the Chinese in the southern lands, all too often saw what they expected to see. This should not really be a cause for surprise or mockery, for it may well be that the human mind has an inherent need to fall back on the familiar object and the standard image, in order to come to terms with the shock of the unfamiliar. The real test comes later, with the capacity to abandon the life-belt which links the unknown to the known. Some Europeans, and especially those who spent a long time in the Indies, did successfully pass this test. Their own dawning realization of the wide divergence between the image and the reality, gradually forced them to abandon their standard images and their inherited preconceptions. For America was a *new* world and a *different* world; and it was this fact of difference which was overwhelmingly borne in upon those who came to know it. 'Everything is very different', wrote Fray Tomás de Mercado in his book of advice to the merchants of Seville; 'the talent of the natives, the disposition of the republic, the method of government and even the capacity to be governed'.[1]

But how to convey this fact of difference, the uniqueness of America, to those who had not seen it? The problem of description reduced writers and chroniclers to despair. There was too much diversity, too many new things to be described, as Fernández de Oviedo constantly complained. 'Of all the things I have seen', he wrote of a bird of brilliant plumage, 'this is the one which has most left me without hope of being able to describe it in words.' Or again of a strange tree—'it needs to be painted by the hand of a Berruguete or some other excellent painter like him, or by Leonardo da Vinci or Andrea Mantegna, famous painters whom I knew in Italy'.[2] But the sheer impossibility of the task itself represented a challenge which could extend the boundaries of perception. Forcing themselves to communicate something of their own delight in what they saw around them, the Spanish chroniclers of the Indies occasionally achieved a pen-picture of startling intimacy and brilliance. What could be more vivid than Las Casas's description of himself reading

---

[1] *Summa de Tratos y Contratos* (Seville, 1571), p. 91.
[2] *Historia General*, i, 158 and 175; ii, 7.

matins 'in a breviary with tiny print' by the light of the Hispaniola fireflies?[1]

Yet there are times when the chroniclers seem cruelly hampered by the inadequacies of their vocabulary; and it is particularly noticeable that the range of colours identifiable by sixteenth-century Europeans seems strictly limited. Again and again travellers express their astonishment at the greenness of America, but can get no further. Just occasionally, as with Sir Walter Raleigh in Guiana, the palette comes to life: 'We sawe birds of all colours, some carnation, some crimson, orenge tawny, purple, greene, watched [i.e. light blue], and of all other sorts both simple and mixt . . .'[2] Jean de Léry, too, can give some idea of the brilliance of plumage of the tropical birds of Brazil. But Léry possesses a quite unusual capacity for putting himself in the position of a European who has never crossed the Atlantic and is forced to envisage the New World from travellers' accounts. He instructs his readers, for instance, how to conceive of a Brazilian savage. 'Imagine in your mind a naked, well-formed and well-proportioned man, with all the hair on his body plucked out . . . his lips and cheeks pierced by pointed bones or green stones, pendants hanging from his pierced ears, his body painted . . . his thighs and legs blackened with dye . . .' Yet even Léry admits defeat in the end. 'Their gestures and countenances are so different from ours, that I confess to my difficulty in representing them in words, or even in pictures. So, to enjoy the real pleasure of them, you will have to go and visit them in their country.'[3]

Pictures, as Léry implied, could aid the imagination. Trained artists who accompanied expeditions to the Indies—like John White, on the Roanoke voyage of 1585, and Frans Post, who followed Prince John Maurice of Nassau to Brazil in 1637—might at least hope to capture something of the New World for those who had not seen it. But the problems of the artist resembled those of the chronicler. His European background and training were likely to determine the nature of his vision; and the techniques and the colour

---

[1] Bartolomé de Las Casas, *Apologética Historia Sumaria*, ed. Edmundo O'Gorman (2 vols. Mexico, 1967), i, 16.
[2] *The Discoverie of the Large, Rich and Bewtiful Empyre of Guiana* (London, 1596), p. 45.
[3] *Voyage fait en la Terre du Bresil*, pp. 176, 119–20, 127.

range with which he had familiarized himself at home were not necessarily adequate to represent the new and often exotic scenes which he now set out to record. Frans Post, trained in the sober Dutch tradition, and carefully looking down the wrong end of his telescope to secure a concentrated field of vision, did manage to capture a fresh, if somewhat muted, image of the New World during his stay in Brazil. But once he was back in Europe, with its own tastes and expectations, the vision began to fade.[1]

Even where the observer depicted a scene with some success, either in paint or in prose, there was no guarantee that his work would reach the European public in an accurate form, or in any form at all. The caprice of publishers and the obsession of governments with secrecy, meant that much information about the New World, which might have helped to broaden Europe's mental horizons, failed to find its way into print. Illustrations had to run further hazards peculiar to themselves. The European reader was hardly in a position to obtain a reliable picture of life among the Tupinambá savages of Brazil when the illustrations in his book included scenes of Turkish life, because the publisher happened to have them in stock. Nor was the technique of woodcuts sufficiently advanced, at least until the second half of the sixteenth century, to allow a very faithful reproduction of the original drawing. Above all, the existence of a middleman between the artist and his public could all too easily distort and transform the image he was commissioned to reproduce. Readers dependent on De Bry's famous engravings for their image of the American Indian could be forgiven for assuming that the forests of America were peopled by heroic nudes, whose perfectly proportioned bodies made them first cousins of the ancient Greeks and Romans.[2]

In spite of all the problems involved in the dissemination of accurate information about America, the greatest problem of all, however, remained that of comprehension. The expectations of the

---

[1] For White, see the magnificent edition of *The American Drawings of John White* by Paul Hulton and D. B. Quinn (2 vols. London, 1964). For the career and techniques of Post, see Erik Larsen, *Frans Post* (Amsterdam–Rio de Janeiro, 1962).

[2] Mumford Jones, *O Strange New World*, pp. 28–32; Atkinson, *Les Nouveaux Horizons*, p. 6; Hans Staden, *The True History of his Captivity*, ed. M. Letts (London, 1928), p. xvii.

European reader, and hence of the European traveller, were formed out of the accumulated images of a society which had been nurtured for generations on tales of the fantastic and the marvellous. When Columbus first set eyes on the inhabitants of the Indies, his immediate reaction was that they were not in any way monstrous or physically abnormal. It was a natural enough reaction for a man who still half belonged to the world of Mandeville.[1]

The temptation was almost overpoweringly strong to see the newly-discovered lands in terms of the enchanted isles of medieval fantasy.[2] But it was not only the fantastic that tended to obtrude itself between the European and reality. If the unfamiliar were to be approached as anything other than the extraordinary and the monstrous, then the approach must be conducted by reference to the most firmly established elements in Europe's cultural inheritance. Between them, therefore, the Christian and the classical traditions were likely to prove the obvious points of departure for any evaluation of the New World and its inhabitants.

In some respects, both of these traditions could assist Europeans in coming to terms with America. Each provided a possible norm or yardstick, other than those immediately to hand in Renaissance Europe, by which to judge the land and the peoples of the newly-discovered world. Some of the more obvious categories for classifying the inhabitants of the Antilles were clearly inapplicable. These people were not monstrous; and their hairlessness made it difficult to identify them with the wild men of the popular medieval tradition.[3] Nor were they Negroes or Moors, the races best known to medieval Christendom. In these circumstances, it was natural for Europeans to look back into their own traditions, and seek to evaluate the puzzling world of the Indies by reference to the Garden of Eden or the Golden Age of antiquity.

The reverence of late medieval Europeans for their Christian and classical traditions had salutary consequences for their approach to

[1] Letter on the first voyage, in *The Journal of Christopher Columbus*, trans. Cecil Jane, ed. L. A. Vigneras (London, 1960), p. 200. For the detachment and realism with which Columbus observed the Caribs, see Olschki, 'What Columbus Saw', and Margaret Hodgen, *Early Anthropology*, pp. 17–20.
[2] L. Olschki, *Storia Letteraria delle Scoperte Geografiche* (Florence, 1937), pp. 39–40.
[3] See Richard Bernheimer, *Wild Men in the Middle Ages* (Cambridge, Mass., 1952).

the New World, in that it enabled them to set it into some kind of perspective in relation to themselves, and to examine it with a measure of tolerant interest. But against these possible advantages must be set certain obvious disadvantages, which in some ways made the task of assimilation appreciably harder. Fifteenth-century Christendom's own sense of self-dissatisfaction found expression in the longing for a return to a better state of things. The return might be to the lost Christian paradise, or to the Golden Age of the ancients, or to some elusive combination of both these imagined worlds. With the discovery of the Indies and their inhabitants, who went around naked and yet—in defiance of the Biblical tradition—mysteriously unashamed, it was all too easy to transpose the ideal world from a world remote in time to a world remote in space. Arcadia and Eden could now be located on the far shores of the Atlantic.[1]

The process of transposition began from the very moment that Columbus first set eyes on the Caribbean Islands. The various connotations of paradise and the Golden Age were present from the first. Innocence, simplicity, fertility and abundance—all of them qualities for which Renaissance Europe hankered, and which seemed so unattainable—made their appearance in the reports of Columbus and Vespucci, and were eagerly seized upon by their enthusiastic readers. In particular, they struck an answering chord in two worlds, the religious and the humanist. Despairing of the corruption of Europe and its ways, it was natural that certain members of the religious orders should have seen an opportunity for reestablishing the primitive church of the apostles in a New World as yet uncorrupted by European vices. In the revivalist and apocalyptic tradition of the friars, the twin themes of the new world and the end of the world harmoniously blended in the great task of evangelizing the uncounted millions who knew nothing of the Faith.[2]

---

[1] For primitivism and utopianism in European thought, see especially H. Baudet, *Paradise on Earth* (New Haven–London, 1965), pp. 34–5.

[2] M. Bataillon, 'Novo Mundo e fim do Mundo', *Revista de História* (São Paulo), no. 18 (1954), pp. 343–51; Charles L. Sanford, *The Quest for Paradise. Europe and the American Moral Imagination* (Urbana, Ill., 1961), pp. 38–40; J. A. Maravall, 'La Utopia político-religiosa de los Franciscanos en Nueva España', *Estudios Americanos*, i (1949), 199–227.

The uncertain impact

The humanists, like the friars, projected onto America their disappointed dreams. In the *Decades* of Peter Martyr, the first popularizer of America and its myth, the Indies have already undergone their subtle transmutation. Here were a people who lived without weights and measures and 'pestiferous moneye, the seed of innumerable myscheves. So that if we shall not be ashamed to confesse the truthe, they seem to lyve in the goulden worlde of the which owlde wryters speake so much: wherin men lyved simplye and innocentlye without inforcement of lawes, without quarrelling Iudges and libelles, contente onely to satisfie nature, without further vexation for knowlege of thinges to come.'[1]

It was an idyllic picture, and the humanists made the most of it, for it enabled them to express their deep dissatisfaction with European society, and to criticize it by implication. America and Europe became antitheses—the antitheses of innocence and corruption. And the corrupt was destroying the innocent. In his recently discovered *History of the Discovery of the Indies*, written in 1528, Pérez de Oliva makes the Indian *caciques* express their plight in speeches that might have been written for them by Livy.[2] By emphasizing their fortitude and nobility of character, he effectively points the contrast between the innocence of the alleged barbarians, and the barbarism of their supposedly civilized conquerors. It was a device which was employed at almost the same moment by another Spanish humanist, who may also have been thinking of the horrors of the conquest—Antonio de Guevara in his famous story of the Danube peasant.[3] As Sir Thomas More had already shown, the overseas discoveries could be used to suggest fundamental questions about the values and the standards of a civilization which was perhaps beyond reform.

But by treating the New World in this way, the humanists were closing the door to understanding an alien civilization. America was not as they imagined it; and even the most enthusiastic of them had

[1] *Decades*, trans. Richard Eden (1555), in *The First Three English Books on America*, ed. Edward Arber (Birmingham, 1885), p. 71.
[2] *Invención de las Yndias*, pp. 94-5, 104-10. See also L. Olschki, 'Hernán Pérez de Oliva's "Ystoria de Colón" ', *Hispanic American Historical Review*, xxiii (1943), 165-96.
[3] Antonio de Guevara, *El Villano del Danubio y otros Fragmentos*, ed. Américo Castro (Princeton, 1945).

to accept from an early stage that the inhabitants of this idyllic world could also be vicious and bellicose, and sometimes ate each other. This of itself was not necessarily sufficient to quench utopianism, for it was always possible to build Utopia on the far side of the Atlantic if it did not already exist. For a moment it seemed as if the dream of the friars and the humanists would find its realization in Vasco de Quiroga's villages of Santa Fe in Mexico.[1] But the dream was a European dream, which had little to do with the American reality. As that reality came to impinge at an increasing number of points, so the dream began to fade.

[1] Silvio Zavala, *Sir Thomas More in New Spain* (Hispanic and Luso-Brazilian Councils, London, 1955); F. B. Warren, *Vasco de Quiroga and his Pueblo-Hospitals of Santa Fe* (Academy of American Franciscan History, Washington, 1963).

2

THE PROCESS OF ASSIMILATION

The New World, as conceived by late medieval and early Renaissance Europeans, proved all too often to be no more than a fragile construct of the mind. The *conquistadores*, who had been driven forward by their greed for booty, land and lordship, watched in dismay as the officials of the Spanish Crown encroached on their feudal paradise. The friars, who had glimpsed in the New World their New Jerusalem, grew progressively disenchanted at the spiritual and moral backslidings of its captive citizens. The Utopia of the humanists, like the Seven Cities of the explorers, seemed increasingly remote and increasingly unreal. By the middle of the sixteenth century the discrepancies between the image and the reality could no longer be systematically ignored. Too many awkward facts were beginning to obtrude.

The assimilation of these facts was to take Europe a century or more. It proved to be a difficult, as well as a lengthy, process; and in many respects it was still far from completed by the middle of the seventeenth century, if we take as our criterion the words of Professor Winch: 'Seriously to study another way of life is necessarily to seek to extend our own—not simply to bring the other way within the already existing boundaries of our own . . .'[1] Applying these words to the general problem involved in coming to terms with the New World as a whole, we are likely to find that the degree of success in sixteenth- and early seventeenth-century Europe was only relative. Much effort went into bringing the known facts about America within the existing boundaries. But even by the middle years of the seventeenth century, the boundaries themselves had barely begun to move.

Given the implications of certain aspects of the discovery of America, this may seem a disappointing outcome for a hundred and fifty years of intellectual endeavour. Guicciardini, with his usual

[1] See above, p. 15.

shrewdness, noted these implications when he wrote: 'Not only has this navigation confounded many affirmations of former writers about terrestrial things, but it has also given some anxiety to interpreters of the Holy Scriptures . . .'[1] Yet even by the mid-seventeenth century the explosive potentialities already glimpsed in the early sixteenth had scarcely begun to be realized. In spite of the problems raised by the growing knowledge of America, no sustained attack had yet been mounted on the historical and chronological accuracy of the Biblical story of the creation of man and his dispersion following the flood. European political and social philosophy was still almost untouched by the results of ethnographical observation and inquiry.[2] The possibilities of relativism as a weapon for challenging long-established religious, political and social assumptions has as yet barely been grasped.

It was only in the century after 1650 that Europe's traditional mental boundaries began to be extended at these crucial points. Before then, we are likely to find little more than isolated reconnaissances outside the stockade, or dramatic advances which are never quite consolidated. But this apparent failure should not blind us to the magnitude of the work that was being undertaken within the stockade in the preceding years. This work was the essential preliminary to any sustained break-out by the garrison. New possibilities had at least been glimpsed, new lines of advance prepared.

To watch the process by which sixteenth-century Europe came to grips with the realities of America is to see something of the character of sixteenth-century European civilization itself, in its strength and in its weakness. Certain elements in Europe's cultural inheritance made it difficult to assimilate new facts and new impressions, but others may have given it certain advantages in confronting a challenge of this magnitude. It was, for instance, important that the European attitude to the scope and purposes of knowledge should have allowed considerable latitude to speculative inquiry. Gregorio García, a Spanish Dominican who published in 1607 a massive

[1] *Storia d'Italia*, ed. Panigada, ii, p. 132 (Bk. vi, c. ix).
[2] This is one of the points made by John H. Rowe, 'Ethnography and Ethnology in the Sixteenth Century', *The Kroeber Anthropological Society Papers*, no. 30 (1964), 1–19. I have found this paper particularly helpful in working on some of the points contained in this chapter.

survey of the numerous hypotheses that had been advanced to explain the origins of the native inhabitants of America, observed that man's knowledge of any given fact derived from one or other of four distinct sources. Two of these sources were infallible: divine faith, as revealed through the scriptures, and *ciencia*, which explained a phenomenon by its cause. But that which was known by human faith rested solely on the authority of its source; and what was known only by opinion must be regarded as uncertain, because it was based on arguments which could well be disproved. The question of the origin of the American Indians came into this last category, because there could be no clear proof, the matter was not discussed in the scriptures, and the problem was too recent to have allowed the amassing of any corpus of convincing authority.[1]

If certain areas, therefore, were fixed and determined for all time by divine pronouncement, there were other areas where the inhabitants of Christendom could range more or less at will. It was important, too, that the pursuit of knowledge should have enjoyed the sanction both of classical antiquity and of Christian doctrine. Quoting, consciously or unconsciously, from Aristotle, Cortés grandly announced in a letter to an oriental potentate that it was 'a universal condition of men to want to know'. The whole European movement of exploration and discovery was informed by this desire to see and to know; and no man better exemplified Aristotle's dictum than Cortés himself, as he probed into the mysteries of volcanoes, observed with fascination the customs of the Indians, and, in his own words, diligently inquired into the 'secrets of these parts'.[2]

Some of this curiosity can be seen as a desire for the acquisition of information for its own sake. The sixteenth century collected facts as it collected exotic objects, assembling them for display in cosmographies like so many curios in a cabinet. But curiosity also had its due place within a wider, Christian, framework. At the end of the century, José de Acosta, in his great *Natural and Moral History of the Indies*, likened men to ants in their refusal to let themselves be deterred, once they had set out on their quest for facts. 'And the high and eternal wisdom of the Creator uses this natural curiosity of men

[1] *Origen de los Indios del Nuevo Mundo y Indias Occidentales* (Valencia, 1607), pp. 17–21.
[2] Cortés, *Cartas y Documentos*, pp. 478 and 202.

to communicate the light of His holy gospel to peoples who still live in the darkness of their errors.'[1] This assumption, that all knowledge was subordinated to a higher purpose and fitted into a providential design, was crucial for the assimilation of the New World of America by sixteenth-century Christendom. Here again, a comparison with the Chinese approach to the southern lands, as described by Professor Schafer, provides a revealing insight. 'Faced with the abnormal world of Nam-Viet', he writes, 'the northerner lacked the help of any generally accepted world view, to which he could optimistically assimilate the unpalatable facts of the south. The Hua man of the T'ang period could not call with complacency on such metaphysical principles as 'order', 'harmony', 'unity in diversity' or even 'beauty'—all conceptions agreeable to our own tradition—to lubricate his difficult adjustment.'[2]

Sixteenth-century Europeans, on the other hand, instinctively accepted the idea of a designed world into which America—however unexpected its first appearance—must somehow be incorporated.[3] Everything that could be known about America must have its place in the universal scheme. Knowledge of the new lands and new peoples could, as Acosta suggested, further the great task of the evangelization of mankind. Knowledge of its infinite diversity, on which Fernández de Oviedo and Las Casas exclaimed with awe and wonder, could only enhance man's appreciation of the omnipotence of its divine creator. Knowledge of the medicinal and therapeutic properties of its plants and herbs was further testimony to God's care for the well-being of His children—and in this context it was particularly reassuring that the New World, having inflicted upon Europe the terrible scourge of syphilis, should conveniently provide a cure, in the form of lignum-vitae.[4] Often, no doubt, the more strictly metaphysical considerations receded far into the background, but there always remained the hard deposit of an engrained conviction that knowledge had a purpose.

[1] *Historia Natural y Moral de las Indias*, ed. Edmundo O'Gorman (2nd ed. Mexico, 1962), p. 112.
[2] *The Vermilion Bird*, p. 115.
[3] For the idea of the designed world in Western thought, see Clarence J. Glacken, *Traces on the Rhodian Shore* (Berkeley, 1967).
[4] Fernández de Oviedo, *Historia General*, i, 53.

31

The process of assimilation

Both approaches to knowledge, the curious and the utilitarian, possessed obvious limitations as a means for broadening the mental horizons of sixteenth-century Europeans. It was of great importance that they should have accepted the fact of the diversity of mankind, and have been stimulated by their reading of classical authors to display a lively curiosity about the habits of different peoples. But the collecting instinct encouraged a tendency towards the indiscriminate accumulation of random ethnographic facts, which made it difficult to establish any coherent pattern of ideas. In some respects it was particularly unfortunate that the sixteenth century possessed an obvious classical model in Pliny's *Natural History*. The often inchoate impression created by Oviedo's *History of the Indies* is partly the outcome of an excessive respect for an authority whose methods were among those least needed by sixteenth-century seekers after truth.[1]

The indiscriminate compilation of facts lumped them together into an undifferentiated category of the marvellous or exotic. This inevitably reduced their effectiveness as vehicles for change. Some were successfully assimilated into pre-existing patterns, while others, which might have been more challenging, remained mere curiosities. Dürer gazed in wonder on Montezuma's treasures, but these exotic objects were curiosities to be admired, not models to be imitated. As the handiwork of 'barbarians', the artistic creations of the peoples of America exercised virtually no influence on sixteenth-century European art. They were simply consigned to the cabinets of collectors—mute witnesses to the alien customs of non-European man.[2]

Many of the *natural* products of America, on the other hand, were more easily accepted and absorbed, especially those which could be put to some practical use. But a rigorously utilitarian approach could be as constricting in its way as indiscriminate collection for curiosity's sake. A concentration on the merely useful inevitably meant that much was omitted or ignored. Yet ultimately it was the stimulus of practical considerations—the need to exploit the resources

[1] For Oviedo's acknowledged indebtedness to Pliny, see for example the *Historia General*, ii, 56.
[2] Nicole Dacos, 'Présents Américains à la Renaissance. L'Assimilation de l'Exotisme', *Gazette des Beaux-Arts*, VIe période, lxxiii (1969), 57–64.

of America and to govern and convert its peoples—which compelled Europeans to widen their field of vision (sometimes in spite of themselves) and to organize and classify their findings within a coherent frame of thought.

Officials and missionaries alike found that, to do their work effectively, they needed some understanding of the customs and traditions of the peoples entrusted to their charge. Royal officials who came from Spain were used to thinking in legal and historical terms, and it was natural enough that they should have applied these to their new environment. How else, for example, could they determine the tax obligations of an Indian to his *encomendero*, other than by first discovering the amount of tribute he used to pay to his native lord in pre-conquest times? The *visitas* of royal officials to Indian localities therefore tended to turn into elaborate inquiries into native history, land tenure and inheritance laws; and the reports of the more intelligent and inquiring of these officials, like Alonso de Zorita in New Spain,[1] were in effect exercises in applied anthropology, capable of yielding a vast amount of information about native customs and society.

In the years immediately following the conquest, missionaries were less concerned than royal officials with the gathering of data. The first generation of missionaries, buoyed up by their faith in the natural innocence and predisposition to goodness of the native inhabitants, assumed that their minds were, in Las Casas's words, *tablas rasas*[2] on which the true faith could easily be inscribed. Bitter experience soon showed otherwise. In his *History of the Indies of New Spain* (1581), the Dominican Fray Diego Durán insisted that there could be no hope of abolishing idolatry among the Indians 'unless we are informed about all the kinds of religion which they practised ... And therefore a great mistake was made by those who, with much zeal but little prudence, burnt and destroyed at the beginning all their ancient pictures. This left us so much in the dark that they can practise idolatry before our very eyes.'[3] This realization that successful missionary enterprise was impossible without some

---

[1] English translation by Benjamin Keen, *The Lords of New Spain* (London, 1965).
[2] *Apologética Historia*, ii, 262.
[3] *Historia de las Indias de Nueva España*, ed. José F. Ramírez (2nd ed. Mexico, 1951), ii, 71.

understanding of native life and ways of thought, was at once the stimulus and the justification for the great studies of pre-conquest history, religion and society undertaken by the members of the religious orders in the later sixteenth century. 'It is not only useful but essential', wrote Acosta, 'that Christians . . . should know the errors and superstitions of former times.'[1]

The strictly practical considerations which governed these missionary inquiries inevitably had certain limiting results. The religious were not interested in studying native society for its own sake, but only as a means of incorporating it as quickly and as completely as possible into what Oviedo called 'the Christian republic'.[2] Given their overriding determination to extirpate abominable and idolatrous practices, it was natural that sympathetic understanding of native civilization should stop abruptly at those points where the Indians had surrendered themselves irrevocably to the devil and his works. Christianity, for instance, precluded a dispassionate approach to the problem of cannibalism—although Las Casas, if he could not excuse it, derived some satisfaction from the fact that cannibalism had also had its devotees in ancient Ireland.[3]

Even if some elements in native civilization defied comprehension, the very effort to acquire a deeper knowledge and understanding of that civilization forced the friars to undertake investigations which brought them up against the boundaries of conventional disciplines and methods. It was necessary for them to learn native languages; and this in turn drove them to compile dictionaries and grammars, like the first grammar of the Quechua language, which was published in 1560 by the Dominican Fray Domingo de Santo Tomás.[4] Language enabled them to explore Indian culture and religion. But, having shaped this tool with considerable difficulty, they then came up against a further, and unexpected, problem—that of evidence.

The nature of this problem is illuminated in a remarkable exchange of letters between Acosta and his fellow-Jesuit Juan de Tovar, who had sent him the manuscript of a history of Mexico. Acosta, in thanking for the manuscript, asked Tovar for assurance on three points which were troubling him. First, 'what certainty or

[1] *Historia Natural y Moral*, p. 278. [2] *Historia General*, ii, 29.
[3] *Apologética Historia*, ii, 354. [4] *Crónicas Peruanas*, ed. F. Esteve Barba, p.x.

authority does this history have?' Second, how did the Indians succeed in preserving for so long, without the art of writing, the memory of so many different events? Third, how could one guarantee the authenticity of the Aztec speeches recorded by Tovar, 'since without the art of writing, it would seem impossible to preserve speeches of such elegance and length'? Tovar, in his reply, explained how young Aztecs were trained to remember and hand on to succeeding generations the great speeches in their national history, and how they made use of pictographic records as aids to memory.[1]

A dependence on oral tradition may not have inspired great confidence among Europeans accustomed to written records, but at least the idea was not wholly foreign to them. Fernández de Oviedo, considering the same question a generation before Acosta, shrewdly reminded his readers that the Castilians, too, had their oral history, in the form of their great romances.[2] There was also an important classical precedent in the histories of Herodotus, whose methods and reliability were the subject of animated debate in the sixteenth century.[3] Herodotus, when investigating the history of foreign and barbarous peoples, had drawn his information from oral tradition. It was therefore possible for sixteenth-century Spaniards to rely on popular memory in compiling their histories of the peoples of America without feeling that they were doing excessive violence to their conception of proper historical method. But their concern for the authenticity of their evidence induced them to refine and develop their techniques of inquiry; and in the hands of an expert like Bernardino de Sahagún the collection of oral evidence became a highly sophisticated piece of ethnographical field-work.

The impact of these methods on sixteenth-century Europe was unfortunately blunted by the fact that so many of the great studies of native culture and society remained unpublished. The works of Durán and Sahagún did not appear in print until the nineteenth

[1] Juan de Tovar, *Historia de la Venida de los Yndios a poblar a Mexico de las partes remotas de Occidente* (*c.* 1583). An edition of the manuscript in the John Carter Brown Library, Providence, Rhode Island, is now being prepared. The correspondence between Tovar and Acosta was printed as document no. 65 in Joaquín García Icazbalceta, *Don Fray Juan de Zumárraga* (1881. New ed. Mexico, 1947, iv, 89-93).
[2] *Historia General*, i, 114-15.
[3] A. D. Momigliano, 'The Place of Herodotus in the History of Historiography', *History*, 43 (1958), 1-13.

century, and Tovar's history of Mexico, which provoked Acosta's questions, remains unpublished to this day. All too often, Europe remained in ignorance of the pioneering methods and the novel findings of those who worked among the native peoples of America. It is not therefore surprising if the evidence for a direct influence on Europe of pioneering techniques developed in America turns out to be scanty. It is also, by its nature, difficult to interpret. Apparent cases of direct influence tend to be ambiguous. The original impetus behind some new departure is as likely as not to be European, although American experience may well provide an additional stimulus.

In the realm of philology, for instance, Garcilaso de la Vega seems to have derived his scholarly interest in the proper spelling of Quechua words from his membership of a circle of Córdoba *savants*, who had learnt from the historian Ambrosio de Morales to employ literary, topographical and philological evidence in their study of Spanish antiquities. But Garcilaso's intimate knowledge of the New World and its history did help to widen the horizons of these anti- quaries. When his friend Bernardo Aldrete published in 1606 his history of the Castilian language, he used the examples of Quechua and Nahuatl to illustrate the way in which military conquest can promote linguistic unity.[1]

American experience may have had a rather more direct, although still limited, impact on methods of governmental inquiry. The need to obtain authentic information about a totally unknown world forced the Spanish Crown to arrange for the collecting of evidence on a massive scale. In this process, the questionnaire became an essential instrument of government. Spanish officials in the Indies were bombarded with questionnaires. The most famous of these (although by no means the earliest) were the ones drafted in the early 1570s at the instigation of the president of the Council of the Indies, Juan de Ovando, to elicit a large amount of detailed information on the geography, the climate, the produce and the inhabitants of Spain's American possessions. There was no obvious reason why a method

---

[1] Bernardo Aldrete, *Del Origen y Principio de la Lengua Castellana* (Rome, 1606), p. 144; José Durand, 'Dos Notas sobre el Inca Garcilaso', *Nueva Revista de Filología Hispánica*, iii (1949), 278–90; Eugenio Asensio, 'Dos Cartas Desconocidas del Inca Garcilaso', *ibid.* vii (1953), 583–93.

of inquiry designed for the New World should not be applied in the Old World too; and in 1574, after Juan de Ovando had moved to the presidency of the Council of Finance, a similar investigation was launched in Castile.[1]

Ovando's initiative suggests how decisive could be the action of a single individual in a key position, but it also reflects a more general aspiration of the age to order and to classify. By the later sixteenth century, as a result of the vast amount of fresh observation during the preceding decades, the problem of classification was becoming acute in every field of knowledge.[2] Knowledge about America was no exception. Large quantities of ill-assorted data about the New World had now found their way to Europe; and there were many manuscripts in private circulation or in the hands of the Council of the Indies, which needed sifting and collating. The overwhelming need by 1570 was for the introduction of method, in a field where investigation was all too often unsystematic, and dependent on the individual efforts of enthusiasts. Fernández de Oviedo had made heroic efforts in his time to embrace the totality of knowledge about the New World in one vast encyclopaedic survey, but a new and more sophisticated generation was beginning to find his methods inadequate. It was somehow symbolic of the amateur approach of Oviedo, that he should have taken every precaution for the safe despatch of a live iguana from Hispaniola to his friend Ramusio in Venice, but omitted to inform himself adequately about its dietary habits. He gave it a barrel of earth for its sustenance, and the unfortunate creature died on the voyage.[3]

The aspiration after a greater professionalism and a higher degree of system expressed itself in many ways in the years around 1570. In 1565 the Sevillan doctor, Nicolás Monardes, published his famous survey of the medicinal plants of America, which appeared

[1] For Ovando and the whole question of the *Relaciones*, see the long introduction (1881, reprinted in Biblioteca de Autores Espanoles, 1965, with further critical discussion by José Urbano Martínez Carreras) by Jiménez de la Espada to the *Relaciones Geográficas de las Indias. Perú.* Also Howard F. Cline, 'The *Relaciones Geográficas* of the Spanish Indies, 1577-1586', *Hispanic American Historical Review*, xliv (1964), 341-74, which includes a complete English translation of the printed questionnaire of 1577.
[2] For the general problem of classification and method in sixteenth-century thought, see Emile Callot, *La Renaissance des Sciences de la Vie au XVIe Siècle* (Paris, 1951).
[3] *Historia General*, ii, 35.

in John Frampton's English translation of 1577 under the title of *Joyfull Newes out of the Newe Founde Worlde*. At about the same time a Bolognese naturalist, Ulisse Aldrovandi, was creating a botanical garden and museum, for both of which he was constantly soliciting specimens from America. Concerned about the lack of method in such books about America as were available to him, he asked the Grand Duke of Tuscany in 1569 to seek permission for him to lead a scientific expedition to the Indies. The permission never came, but two years later Philip II did dispatch just such an expedition to America under the leadership of the Spanish naturalist and physician Dr Francisco Hernández.[1]

In 1571, the same year as Hernández left for Mexico, the Spanish Crown created a new post, that of cosmographer and official chronicler of the Indies, and appointed to it Juan López de Velasco, a close associate of the reforming president of the Council of the Indies, Juan de Ovando.[2] There was a dual intention behind the establishment of this post: to provide an exact record of the Spanish achievement in America in the face of foreign calumnies, and to reduce the shameful ignorance of the councillors of the Indies about the lands under their jurisdiction. In practice, the official *history* of the Indies had to wait until a later chronicler, Antonio de Herrera, published his *Decades* in the early seventeenth century. But Velasco, whose own interests seem to have been more cosmographical than historical, duly wrote between 1571 and 1574 a *Geography and Universal Description of the Indies*.[3] This was exactly the kind of work that was needed at this moment—a brilliantly succinct and lucid synthesis of the existing information on the geography, the natural phenomena and the peoples of the Indies. But Velasco's work, like the voluminous botanical notes of Hernández, remained virtually unknown to contemporaries, and was not published in full until 1894. Once again, an important contribution to knowledge was deprived of its rightful impact by its failure to appear in print.

[1] Mario Cermentati, 'Ulisse Aldrovandi e l'America', *Annali di Botanica*, iv (Rome, 1906), 313–66.
[2] For the chronicle of the Indies, see Rómulo D. Carbia, *La Crónica Oficial de las Indias Occidentales* (Buenos Aires, 1940).
[3] *Geografía y Descripción Universal de las Indias*, ed. Justo Zaragoza (Madrid, 1894). For Velasco, see also Carbia pp. 144 ff. and Gonzalo Menéndez-Pidal, *Imagen del Mundo Hacia 1570* (Madrid, 1944), pp. 13–15.

Velasco's work, however, although a *tour de force*, was essentially a compendium, and it was not until the publication in Spanish in 1590 of José de Acosta's great *Natural and Moral History of the Indies*, that the process of integrating the American world into the general framework of European thought was at last triumphantly achieved. This History was, Acosta claimed, a novel undertaking. Many authors, he wrote, had described the new and exotic features of the Indies, just as many had described the deeds of the Spanish conquerors. 'But until now I have not come across any author who attempts to explain the causes and the reasons for these novel phenomena of nature . . . nor have I found any book devoted to the history of the original Indian inhabitants, who are native to the New World.'[1] In effect he was engaged in the supremely difficult task of displaying to European readers the unique characteristics of America and its inhabitants, while at the same time emphasizing the underlying unity between the Old World and the New. The competing claims of unity and diversity were reconciled in a synthesis which owed much to the Aristotelian cast of Acosta's thought.

But Acosta's synthesis was itself the culmination of a century of intellectual endeavour, in the course of which three different aspects of the American world were being slowly and painfully assimilated into the European consciousness. America, as an entity in space, had demanded incorporation into Europe's mental image of the natural world. American man had to be found his place among the peoples of mankind. And America, as an entity in time, required integration into Europe's conception of the historical process. All this was achieved during the course of the sixteenth century, and it was Acosta's synthesizing genius which brought the great enterprise to completion.

The gradual acceptance by Europeans of the natural and geographical phenomenon of America was at once hindered and helped by their dependence on the geographical learning of classical antiquity. The challenge to that learning was vividly expressed by the Portuguese Pedro Nunes when he wrote in his *Treatise of the Sphere*, of 1537: 'New islands, new lands, new seas, new peoples;

[1] *Historia Natural y Moral*, p. 13. Edmundo O'Gorman's introduction to his edition of Acosta admirably summarizes the author's intentions and achievement.

39

and, what is more, a new sky and new stars.'[1] It was not easy to break away from the traditional conception of the *orbis terrarum* with its three landmasses of Europe, Asia and Africa, any more than it was easy to break away from the idea of an unnavigable and uninhabitable torrid zone in the southern hemisphere. If experience effectively disproved the second of these theses at an early stage, it did not disprove the first of them until the crossing of the Behring Strait in 1728. It was therefore reasonable enough that there should have been continuing uncertainty throughout the sixteenth-century as to whether or not America formed part of Asia. Las Casas eventually decided that in fact it did,[2] whereas Fernández de Oviedo suspected that 'the mainland of these Indies is another half of the world, as large as, or perhaps larger than, Asia, Africa and Europe . . .'[3]

Certain cosmographical ideas derived from classical antiquity were in fact vindicated by the discoveries. Indeed, the reading of Strabo in conjunction with Ptolemy, together with the evidence provided by Portuguese experience, made it possible for the Florentine Lorenzo Buonincontri to postulate the existence of a fourth continent in 1476.[4] But other ideas—about uninhabitable regions or climatic zones—had to be abandoned or profoundly modified. Nor could classical learning be of any great value in interpreting the phenomena of a part of the world of which it had remained unaware. Here, as Fernández de Oviedo never tired of pointing out, there was no substitute for personal experience. 'What I have said cannot be learnt in Salamanca, Bologna or Paris . . .'[5] The superiority of direct personal observation over traditional authority was proved time and time again in the new environment of America. And on each fresh occasion, another fragment was chipped away from the massive rock of authority.

But the very fact that the natural phenomena of the New World

---

[1] Quoted by Joaquim de Carvalho, *Estudos sobre a cultura portuguesa do século XVI*, i (Coimbra, 1947), 42.
[2] The evidence for this is summarized in Appendix V of O'Gorman's edition of the *Apologética Historia*.
[3] *Historia General*, ii, 86.
[4] Thomas Goldstein, 'Geography in Fifteenth-century Florence', *Merchants and Scholars*, ed. John Parker (Minneapolis, 1965), p. 25.
[5] *Historia General*, i, 39.

did not figure in the traditional cosmographies or natural histories, made it all the harder to bring them within the compass of the European consciousness. One device frequently employed was that of analogy or comparison. But the comparative method had its own dangers and disadvantages. When Oviedo and Las Casas compared Hispaniola to those other two famous islands, England and Sicily, in order to prove that it was in no way inferior to them in fertility, the general effect was simply to blur the differences between all three.[1] Acosta, who saw the danger, specifically warned against the assumption that American species differed accidentally, and not in essence, from those of Europe. The differences were sometimes so great, he said, that to reduce them all to European types was like calling an egg a chestnut.[2]

For Acosta, American nature had its own distinctive characteristics, as belonging to a distinctive fourth part of the world, but it simultaneously partook of enough general characteristics to make it one among the four parts of a common whole. The same, moreover, was as true of man as of nature. 'All things human resemble each other very closely', he wrote, in justification of his decision to devote one of the seven books of his *Natural and Moral History* to the history of the Mexican Indians.[3] But it was precisely this question of the humanity, or the degree of humanity, of the peoples of America which had been the cause of such agitated debate throughout the sixteenth century. For American man, even more than the geographical entity of America, forced upon Europeans a fundamental re-examination of traditional ideas and attitudes.

At the time of the discovery of America, there already existed a number of loosely defined categories into which Europeans could slot the different peoples of the world.[4] The dual inheritance of Europe itself—the Judeo-Christian and the classical—encouraged a dual classification of mankind, whereby peoples were judged in accordance with their religious affiliation or their degree of civility. The fundamental division along religious lines was between Christian and heathen. But Renaissance Europeans also appropriated

[1] *Historia General*, i, 78–82; *Apologética Historia*, i, 95–103.
[2] *Historia Natural y Moral* p. 203.   [3] *Historia Natural y Moral*, p. 319.
[4] Rowe, 'Ethnography and Ethnology'.

from classical literature the distinction between Greeks and barbarians; and the barbarian, while heathen, was also rough and
unpolished. Different peoples displayed different degrees of bar-
barity, and the differences were generally explained by astrological
and environmental influences. Aristotle had taught Europeans to
think of man—and even the most barbarous man—as a naturally
social creature, but it was also recognized that certain men existed
who were so savage or wild as to live solitary lives in the forests,
without benefit of religion or social institutions. Like Nebuchad-
nezzar, the prototype of the wild man, these savages represented
man in his degenerate rather than in his primitive form, although
classical doctrines of the Golden Age had created an awareness
that the solitary forest-dweller could also represent man in a
state of primaeval innocence, before he was corrupted by civil
life.[1]

These general ideas about man and society provided at least a
crude frame of reference which could help Europeans to come to
terms with the peoples of America. But inevitably, over the course of
the sixteenth century, the increased knowledge and understanding of
the indigenous inhabitants of America, and of the vast differences
between them, exposed the inadequacies of the intellectual framework, and forced its modification. From the very beginning, there
were sharp disagreements about the nature of American man. On
the whole, the image of the innocent Indian was most easily maintained by those Europeans who had never actually seen one. Europeans who had experienced any prolonged contact with him were as
likely as not to swing sharply to the other extreme. Commenting on
the diet of the natives of Hispaniola, which included roots, snakes
and spiders, Dr Chanca, who accompanied Columbus on his second
voyage, remarked: 'It seems to me that their bestiality is greater than
that of any beast in the world.'[2] This theme of the bestiality of the
Indian, alternating with the theme of his primaeval innocence, runs
through the early literature of discovery and settlement, although it
is not clear that even the most extreme exponents of the bestial

[1] Bernheimer, *Wild Men*, especially pp. 5–12 and 102.
[2] *Select Documents illustrating the Four Voyages of Columbus*, ed. Cecil Jane (Hakluyt
Society, 2nd series, vol. 65, London, 1930), i, 71.

thesis ever went so far as to deny him all right to the name of man. If he was not a man, then he was incapable of receiving the faith; and it was precisely this capacity for conversion on which Paul III insisted when he proclaimed in the bull *Sublimis Deus* of 1537 that 'the Indians are true men'.[1]

The Christian tradition defined man in terms of his receptivity to divine grace; the classical tradition defined him in terms of his rationality. It was generally accepted, especially after *Sublimis Deus*, that the native peoples of America satisfied the criteria of both these traditions sufficiently to be included among the human kind. But the exact degree to which they satisfied these criteria remained a matter of continuous debate. So far from being peculiarly fitted to receive the pure milk of the gospel, as the first generation of friars had fondly hoped, the Indians gave every sign of extreme religious unreliability. Catholics and Protestants were united on this. Fernández de Oviedo voiced the gravest misgivings about the genuineness of their conversion;[2] and Jean de Léry found ample evidence among the Tupinambá of Brazil for the validity of Calvinist teaching. 'Look at the inconstancy of this poor people, a fine example of the corrupt nature of man.'[3]

The degree of rationality to be found among the Indians was as open to question as their degree of fitness to receive the faith. For Fernández de Oviedo they were clearly inferior beings, naturally idle and inclined to vice; and he found evidence for their inferiority, not in their colour—for colour in the sixteenth century possessed few of the connotations which it later acquired[4]—but in the size and thickness of their skulls, which indicated a deformation in that part of the body which provided an index of a man's rational powers.[5] This assumption indicates that there existed, at least among the

---

1 Lewis Hanke, 'Pope Paul III and the American Indians', *Harvard Theological Review*, xxx (1937), 65–102. See also Lewis Hanke, *Aristotle and the American Indians* (London, 1959), pp. 23–4, and the references there given, for the meaning of *bestia*.
2 *Historia General*, ii, 115.   3 *Voyage fait en la Terre du Bresil*, p. 278.
4 Hodgen, *Early Anthropology*, p. 214. Variations in colour were attributed to length of exposure to the sun. Blackness did, however, possess certain disagreeable connotations, at least for the sixteenth-century Englishman. See Winthrop D. Jordan, *White Over Black* (Chapel Hill, 1968), c. i.
5 *Historia General*, i, 111; Josefina Zoraida Vázquez, 'El Indio americano y su circunstancia en la obra de Fernández de Oviedo', *Revista de Indias*, año XVII, nos. 69–70 (1957), 483–519.

Spanish colonists, a crude biological theory which could be used to underpin Sepúlveda's Aristotelian doctrine of the natural servitude of the Indians on the grounds of their inferiority to the Spaniards as rational beings. 'The Indians', declared an anonymous expert, whose opinion was put forward to Philip III by the official representative of the mining community of New Spain in 1600, 'can be said to be slaves of the Spaniards ... in accordance with the doctrine of Aristotle's *Politics* that those who need to be ruled and governed by others may be called their slaves ... And for this reason Nature specially proportioned their bodies, so that they should have the strength for personal service. The Spaniards, on the other hand, are delicately proportioned, and were made prudent and clever, so that they should be able to lead a political and civil life' (*tratar la policía y urbanidad*).[1]

The equation between bestiality, irrationality and barbarism was easily made; and those who made it could then proceed to draw on Aristotelian doctrine to justify Spanish domination over the Indians as both natural and necessary. Those Spaniards who, like Vitoria, felt the blood run cold in their veins at the thought of the behaviour of their compatriots in the Indies,[2] were therefore driven to reconsider at a new and deeper level the traditional European classification of the peoples of the world. This process of reappraisal was supremely important, because it gradually forced Europeans to move away from a narrow and primarily political definition of 'civility' towards the broader concept of 'civilization', which was not necessarily equated with Christianity.[3]

Fray Tomás de Mercado, writing in the 1560s, called Negroes and Indians 'barbarians' because 'they are never moved by reason, but only by passion'.[4] In order to counter this kind of traditional argument, it was necessary to produce proofs of Indian rationality.

---

[1] *Parecer de un hombre docto ... cerca del servicio personal de los indios ... presentado a la magestad católica por don Alonso de Oñate ...* (Madrid, 1600), f. 4. Printed memorandum (11 folios) in the John Carter Brown Library, Providence.

[2] Letter from Francisco de Vitoria to Padre Arcos (8 November 1534) in Vitoria's *Relectio de Indis*, ed. L. Pereña and J. M. Pérez Prendes (Madrid, 1967), p. 137.

[3] For 'civility' and 'civilization', see Rowe, 'Ethnography and Ethnology', and C. Vivanti, 'Alle origini dell' idea di civiltà: le scoperte geografiche e gli scritti di Henri de la Popelinière', *Rivista Storica Italiana*, lxxiv (1962), 225–49.

[4] *Samma de Tratos*, p. 102.

The very search for these proofs helped to shape the idea of what constituted a civilized man. Las Casas, for instance, pointed to Mexican architecture—'the very ancient vaulted and pyramid-like buildings'—as 'no small index of their prudence and good polity' (a thesis rejected by Sepúlveda on the grounds that bees and spiders could produce artefacts that no man could imitate).[1] But architectural achievement was only one among many indications of capacity for social and political life which deeply impressed many European observers of the American scene. 'There is', wrote Vitoria in the 1530s, 'a certain method in their affairs, for they have polities which are orderly arranged and they have definite marriage and magistrates and overlords, laws, and workshops, and a system of exchange, all of which call for the use of reason; they also have a kind of religion'.[2]

The implications of this, as spelt out by Vitoria, were so far-reaching that they were bound to affect Christendom's conception of its relationship with the outer world. Rationality, measured by the capacity for living in society, was the criterion of civility; and if this civility was not crowned, as it should have been, with Christianity, this tended to be a misfortune rather than a crime. 'It is through no fault of theirs' wrote Vitoria, 'that these aborigines have for many centuries been outside the pale of salvation, in that they have been born in sin and void of baptism and the use of reason whereby to seek out the things needful for salvation. Accordingly I for the most part attribute their seeming so unintelligent and stupid to a bad and barbarous upbringing, for even among ourselves we find many peasants who differ little from brutes.'[3]

Vitoria's argument placed Christianity and barbarism in a new perspective, although it was a perspective which was deeply influenced by Graeco-Roman theories of men as rational beings, who constituted among themselves a world-wide community. The American Indians, by showing their capacity for social existence, had vindicated their right to membership in the club. The club

[1] Las Casas, *Apologética Historia*, ii, 531; Juan Ginés de Sepúlveda, *Demócrates Segundo*, ed. Angel Losada (Madrid, 1951), p. 36.
[2] *De Indis*. Translation by J. B. Scott, *The Spanish Origin of International Law*, part i (Oxford, 1934), Appendix A, p. xiii.
[3] *Ibid.*

could not be reserved for Christians only, for all rational men were citizens of 'the whole world, which in a certain way constitutes a single republic'.[1] If this was so, what became of the traditional distinction between Christian and barbarian? Inevitably it began to be blurred, and its significance as a divisive force to decline.

In his *Relation of the Lords of New Spain*, written some time before 1570, Alonso de Zorita, for example, notes the discrepancy between Cortés's eulogistic descriptions of the achievements of the Aztecs, and his persistent tendency to call them 'barbarians'. The use of the word 'barbarian' in this context may have arisen, he thought, 'from the fact that we are accustomed to calling infidels "barbarians" ', in conformity with the usage of the Psalmist, as in Psalm 114, where the Egyptians are called barbarians because they were idolaters. 'Yet in other respects', as he observed, 'the Egyptians were a very sage people.' He also noted the tendency of the Greeks and Romans to describe as 'barbarian' all those peoples whose language, customs and religious practices differed from their own. 'Again, perhaps the Spaniards call the Indians barbarous on account of their great simplicity, for they are by nature free of duplicity and cunning . . . Because of this great innocence of the Indians, those who trade with them can cheat them very easily . . . But we could also call the Spaniards barbarians in this sense, for at the present day, even in the best-governed cities, little toy swords and horses, and brass whistles, and little wire snakes, and castanets with bells, are sold in the streets . . . Let those who call [the Indians] barbarians consider that by the same token they could call "barbarians" the Spaniards and other peoples famed for great ability and intelligence.'[2] Here already we can see the attitude of mind which would later prompt Montaigne to write those famous words—'everyone calls barbarian what is not his own usage'.[3]

Zorita's discussion of the nature of barbarism suggests how their experience of other peoples was forcing Europeans to see themselves in a new, and sometimes unexpected, light. But this would have been much more difficult, and might never have happened, if

---

[1] *De Potestate Civili*, in *Obras de Francisco de Vitoria*, ed. Teófilo Urdánoz (Biblioteca de Autores Cristianos, vol. 198, Madrid, 1960), p. 191.

[2] (Trans. Keen, Rutgers, 1963; London, 1965), pp. 170–3.

[3] *Essais*, livre i, c. xxxi ('Des Cannibales') (Pléiade ed., Paris, 1950), p. 243.

Europe's own cultural traditions had not included certain elements and characteristics which at least created a predisposition to react in this way. The Judeo-Christian and the classical traditions were sufficiently disparate, and sufficiently rich and varied in themselves, to have brought a large number of different, and often incompatible ideas, into uneasy coexistence within a single frame of thought. Some of these ideas might for long have been recessive, and others dominant. But a sudden external shock, like the discovery of the peoples of America, could upset the prevailing kaleidoscopic pattern and bring alternative ideas, or combinations of ideas, into view. There was, for instance, perfectly good scriptural authority for the relativism implicit in Zorita's approach to barbarism, in the form of a passage from 1 Corinthians (14. 10–11): 'There are, it may be, so many kinds of voices in the world, and none of them is without significance. Therefore if I know not the meaning of the voice, I shall be unto him that speaketh a barbarian, and he that speaketh shall be a barbarian unto me.'

In changing and refining Europe's conception of barbarism and civility, therefore, as in so many other areas of thought, the discovery of America was important, less because it gave birth to totally new ideas, than because it forced Europeans to come face to face with ideas and problems which were already to be found within their own cultural traditions. But those traditions proved rich enough, on exploration, to provide them with answers to at least some of the puzzling questions raised by America. Their veneration for classical antiquity made them aware of the existence of other civilizations which had been superior to their own. Christian and Stoic thought had given them an idea of the fundamental unity of mankind. Aristotle had taught them to think of man as essentially a social being. All this enabled some of them at least to view their own society with a measure of detachment, and to seek to determine the nature of the relationship between themselves and the other peoples of the world, with some degree of success.

In this enterprise the contribution of Aristotelian doctrine proved to be critical. Aristotle may have furnished Sepúlveda with his arguments in favour of the natural inferiority of the Indian; but it was Aristotle, too, who enabled Vitoria to argue for the inalienable

47

prerogatives of heathen societies, and it was the Aristotelian system which made possible the two greatest attempts of the sixteenth century to incorporate America within a unified vision of the world, man, and history—those of Las Casas and Acosta.

Las Casas's massive *Apologética Historia*, probably written during the 1550s, is an unread masterpiece—unread partly because it is nearly unreadable, and partly because it had to wait until the twentieth century to see the light of day. Its neglect is unfortunate because, for all its faults, it represents an extraordinarily ambitious and erudite attempt to embrace the peoples of the New World within a global survey of human civilization. In order to prove his thesis that the Indian is a fully rational being, perfectly equipped both to govern himself and to receive the gospel, Las Casas examines him from both the physical and the moral standpoint, in conformity with the criteria adduced by Aristotle. The results of his analysis of Indian societies can then be compared with those obtained from a similar analysis of the societies of the Old World, and especially (but by no means exclusively) those of the Greeks and the Romans. Las Casas's study therefore becomes a great essay in comparative cultural anthropology, in which the social and religious habits of Greeks, Romans, and Egyptians, ancient Gauls and ancient Britons, are examined alongside those of the Aztecs and the Incas, generally to the advantage of the latter.

But there was one potentially embarrassing problem which Las Casas had to face. He could produce a formidable battery of arguments and examples to prove the complete rationality of those Indian peoples who lived in organized polities. But what of those who were so barbarous that they lived like beasts of the forest? After considering various possible reasons for man to live outside society, such as the settlement of new lands, or the absence of danger from other men or wild beasts, Las Casas found his answer in Cicero's formulation of the Stoic doctrine that 'all the peoples of the world are men; and there is only one definition of each and every man, and that is that he is rational'. If this was so—if man was indeed a rational being—then even the most barbarous of men could in due course, with care and persistence, be induced to live in an ordered polity.[1]

[1] *Apologética Historia*, i, 248 and 257.

48

This argument implied the existence of varying degrees of barbarism and civility; and Las Casas in fact concluded his History by analysing the meaning of 'barbarian', and dividing barbarians into a number of differing types. 'Barbarian' could be used of all those peoples who did not profess the Christian faith, in which case the Indians were barbarians. But 'barbarian' could also be applied to people who were so out of their minds as to behave like brutes; to those who refused to subject themselves to laws and social life; and to those who lacked the art of writing and spoke strange languages. To some extent the Indians might be deemed to come into this last category, although, as far as language was concerned, 'we are just as barbarous to them as they to us.'[1]

This process of classification was taken a stage further by Acosta in his *De Procuranda Indorum Salute*, written in 1576. For Acosta, the highest category of barbarians were those who, like the Chinese and Japanese, lived in stable republics and had magistrates, cities and books. In the middle category were those who lacked the art of writing and 'civil and philosophical knowledge', like the Mexicans and Peruvians, but possessed admirable forms of government. The third and lowest were those peoples who lived 'without king, without compacts, without magistrates or republic, and who changed their dwelling-place, or—if it were fixed—had one that resembled the cave of a wild beast'.[2]

By adopting classifications of this kind, Las Casas and Acosta were in effect re-opening, on the basis of all the fresh evidence from America, a question which had long perplexed and fascinated Europeans—that of cultural diversity.[3] How were the differences between peoples to be explained? The traditional answer, re-formulated for the sixteenth century by Bodin, placed a heavy emphasis on geography and climate. But observation of the peoples of the New World helped to focus attention on alternative explanations, such as the importance of migration. If the inhabitants of America were indeed descendants of Noah, as orthodox thought

---

[1] ii, 637–54.
[2] Trans. and ed. by Francisco Mateos (Madrid, 1952), pp. 46–8.
[3] For the question of cultural diversity, Hodgen, *Early Anthropology*, c. vi; Rowe, 'Ethnography and Ethnology'; Glacken, *Traces on the Rhodian Shore*, part iii, c. 9.

insisted that they must be,[1] it was clear that they must have forgotten the social virtues in the course of their wanderings. Acosta, who held that they came to the New World overland from Asia, believed that they had turned into hunters during their migration. Then, by degrees, some of them collected together in certain regions of America, recovered the habit of social life, and began to constitute polities.[2]

This argument postulated a sequence of development from barbarism to civility. This sequence was clearly stated by Acosta for man in America, but the idea also had implications for the history of Europe which did not go entirely unnoticed. Too little was known about other contemporary non-European societies to allow very elaborate comparisons between them and those of America. But there had been much comparison between American customs and those of past European societies, and this comparison had revealed some striking similarities. The logical deduction was that the sequence was not necessarily confined to America, and that the ancestors of modern Europeans had once been like the present inhabitants of America. The natives of Florida, wrote Las Casas, were still 'in that first rude state which all other nations were in, before there was anyone to teach them . . . We ought to consider what we, and all the other nations of the world were like, before Jesus Christ came to visit us.'[3] And, as if to show, John White's drawings of 1585 of North American Indians were used as the basis for imaginative representations of Ancient Picts and Ancient Britons.[4]

By the end of the sixteenth century, then, the experience of America had provided Europe with at least the faint outlines of a theory of social development. But this theory was set into a general framework of historical thought which was European in its points of reference, and Christian and providentialist in its interpretation of the historical process. The criterion for assessing the development of non-European peoples remained firmly Europocentric. The peoples

[1] Don Cameron Allen, *The Legend of Noah* (Illinois Studies in Language and Literature, vol. xxxiii, nos. 3–4, Urbana, Illinois, 1949).
[2] *Historia Natural y Moral*, pp. 323–4. Also, pp. 63–4.
[3] *Apologética Historia*, i, 260 and 546.
[4] See T. D. Kendrick, *British Antiquity* (London, 1950) pp. 123–5. Dr Peter Burke kindly drew my attention to this reference. The same point is made by Rowe, 'Ethnography and Ethnology'.

of the New World really were *new* peoples, argued Etienne Pasquier when he heard about the Brazilian savages, if you compared their 'rude manners' with the 'civility of our own'.[1] But this civility was itself the outcome of Christianity, which must form the logical culmination and climax of any story of man's ascent from a barbarian state. The Peru of Garcilaso de la Vega, for instance, passes through three clearly defined stages of historical development. Before the coming of the Incas it is a savage and barbarous society, where men live like beasts in utter spiritual darkness. The Inca Empire, bringing with it the glimmerings of natural law and civilization, was the New World equivalent of the Roman Empire, whose establishment was the necessary preliminary for the spread of Christianity. The arrival of the Spaniards bearing the gospel marked the opening of a new and glorious epoch, which could be seen as the climax of God's majestic design for the peoples of Peru.[2]

The Christian and progressive view of history maintained by a Garcilaso or an Acosta contrasted sharply with the historical pessimism of those who clung to the cyclical theory of the rise and fall of civilizations. The almost miraculous sequence of events which led to the discovery, conquest and conversion of the New World did much to reinforce the linear and progressive, as against the cyclical, interpretation of the historical process in sixteenth-century thought.[3] But this linear interpretation was perfectly capable of escaping from its Christian context. The idea of human development from savagery to civilization could easily lead an autonomous life of its own, and be regarded as a purely secular process. The lesson of the contrast between the peoples of America and Europe did not necessarily point in the first place to Christianity. 'Let anyone but consider', wrote Sir Francis Bacon, 'the immense difference between men's lives in the most polished countries of Europe, and in any wild and barbarous region of the new Indies, he will think it so

---

[1] *Œuvres*, vol. ii, bk. iii, letter iii, p. 55.
[2] *Royal Commentaries of the Incas* (trans. H. V. Livermore, 2 vols., Austin, Texas, 1966), i, 30 and 40 ff. (Bk. i, cs. ix and xv). For Garcilaso's view of the historical process, see the essay by Carlos Daniel Valcárcel in *Nuevos Estudios sobre el Inca Garcilaso de la Vega* (Lima, 1955).
[3] This is one of the points made by José Antonio Maravall in the suggestive chapter on 'La circunstancia del descubrimiento de América' in his study of the idea of progress, *Antiguos y Modernos* (Madrid, 1966).

great, that man may be said to be a god unto man, not only on account of mutual aids and benefits, but for their comparative states—the result of the arts, and not of the soil or climate.'[1]

There was evidence enough in the century of European history since the discovery of America to sustain a thesis that the cultivation of the arts was the determinant of progress. And if progress now became a conceivable possibility, this was partly on account of the discoveries themselves. The reverence for antiquity, and the belief in the existence of a Golden Age in the distant past, had both been undermined. The very fact of the discovery of America meant that the moderns had achieved something that had not been achieved by antiquity; and it vividly revealed the value of first-hand experience as against inherited tradition. 'Experience runs counter to philosophy', wrote Gómara in his *History of the Indies*.[2] Because this experience was peculiar to the modern age, it became increasingly necessary to reconsider accepted views about the historical process. 'The age which they call golden', wrote Bodin, 'if it be compared with ours, would seem but iron . . .' Bodin's famous rejection of a Golden Age located somewhere in the past was partly inspired by the discoveries. 'No one, looking closely into this matter, can doubt that the discoveries of our men ought to be compared with the discoveries of our elders; many ought to be placed first.'[3]

If the discovery of the New World, therefore, strengthened the Christian providentialist interpretation of history as a progressive movement which would culminate in the evangelization of all mankind, it equally strengthened the more purely secular interpretation of history as a progressive movement which would culminate in the civilization of all mankind. Recent events had shown the superiority of modern Europeans, at least in some respects, to the men of classical times. But they had also shown their superiority to the barbarous peoples of a sizeable portion of the globe. No doubt there were some qualifications. 'There is no people so barbarous', wrote Acosta, 'that it does not contain some good in it, just as there is no people, however civilized, which does not have something that

---

[1] *Novum Organum* (1620), Aphorism 129.
[2] *Historia General de las Indias*, p. 160
[3] *Method for the Easy Comprehension of History*, trans. Beatrice Reynolds (New York, 1945), pp. 296 and 301.

deserves to be improved.'[1] Some Europeans, horrified by the barbarities committed at home, entertained legitimate doubts about the reality or value of their own 'civilization'. Jean de Léry, back in France, thought nostalgically of his time among the savages of Brazil;[2] and the counter-balancing attractions of civilization and innocence meant that the idea of progress lived an uneasy and precarious life.

Yet the doubts, if not silenced, were effectively held in check by the growing pride in the extent of Modern Europe's accomplishments. In discovering America Europe had discovered itself. The military, spiritual and intellectual conquest of the New World made it aware of its own power and achievements, at the same time as it was becoming aware, in Bodin's words, that 'all men surprisingly work together in a world state, as if in one and the same city-state'.[3] But this *republica mundana* was conceived along European lines, and the New World was admitted to it on European terms. This very fact imposed certain obvious limits on the extent to which the assimilation of America acted as a transforming experience for Europe itself. The Europe of 1600 was confident of itself—more confident than the Europe of a hundred years before. And a confident society does not ask too many questions which may provoke embarrassing answers. This Europe was symbolized, not by the humanist with his illusions and his doubts, but by the portrait of a Spanish captain, Vargas Machuca, whose description of the Indies of 1599[4] showed him in the frontispiece with one hand on his sword, and the other holding a pair of compasses on top of a globe. Beneath was inscribed the motto:

A la espada y el compás   By compasses and by the sword
Más y más y más y más.   More and more and more and more.

By 1600, having conquered America and brought it within the confines of his intellectual world, the European could survey the earth with pride, confident in his own spiritual and technical superiority, his military capacity and his economic power.

---

[1] *Historia Natural y Moral*, p. 319.   [2] *Voyage fait en la Terre du Bresil*, p. 382.
[3] *Method*, p. 301.
[4] Bernardo de Vargas Machuca, *Milicia y Descripción de las Indias* (Madrid, 1599). See frontispiece.

3

THE NEW FRONTIER

The process by which the New World found its place within the mental horizons of Europe was a slow one, and it entailed some measure of disturbance to established patterns of thought. But the disturbance caused by the discovery of America was not restricted to Europe's intellectual life. The New World also had to be incorporated into Europe's economic and political systems; and here, too, the process of incorporation could not be expected to leave Europe as it found it. The economic and social consequences for Europe of America's discovery, however ambiguous and uncertain, are so closely related to the political consequences, that any divorce between them is bound to appear artificial and misleading. But the very uncertainties may be held to justify at least a temporary perpetuation of a divorce which enjoys a certain sanction in Europe's historiographical tradition, even though, in the last analysis, no clear dividing line can, or should, be drawn.

There is indeed a distinguished line of historical thought which seeks to explain and interpret the economic development of modern Europe by reference to the overseas discoveries. Again it is the eighteenth century which provides the first generalized statements of an 'American' interpretation of modern European history. The Abbé Raynal asserted that the discovery of the New World and of a passage to India by the Cape of Good Hope 'gave rise to a revolution in the commerce, and in the power of nations; and in the manners, industry, and government of the world in general. At this period new connexions were formed by the most distant regions, for the supply of wants they had never before experienced.'[1] Adam Smith presumably had this passage of Raynal in mind when he wrote: 'By uniting, in some measure, the most distant parts of the world, by enabling them to relieve one another's wants, to increase one another's enjoyments, and to encourage one another's industry,

[1] *A Philosophical and Political History* (English trans. 1776), i, 1.

their general tendency would seem to be beneficial.' For Smith, as for Raynal, the long-term consequences of the discovery of America for mankind in general remained obscure; but one of the principal effects, as far as Europe was concerned, had been to 'raise the mercantile system to a degree of splendour and glory which it could never otherwise have attained to . . . In consequence of those discoveries, the commercial towns of Europe, instead of being the manufacturers and carriers for but a very small part of the world . . . have now become the manufacturers for the numerous and thriving cultivators of America, and the carriers, and in some respects the manufacturers too, for almost all the different nations of Asia, Africa and America.'[1]

Some seventy years later, the coolly appraising conclusions of Smith and Raynal were incorporated into a more apocalyptic view of the march of human history. 'The discovery of America, the rounding of the Cape, opened up fresh ground for the rising bourgeoisie. The East-Indian and Chinese markets, the colonization of America, trade with the colonies, the increase in the means of exchange and in commodities generally, gave to commerce, to navigation, to industry, an impulse never before known, and thereby, to the revolutionary element in the tottering feudal society, a rapid development.'[2]

Here, then, is a formulation of modern European history in which the discovery and exploitation of America plays a crucial role in promoting economic and social change. The discovery of America becomes intimately associated with the rise of European capitalism, and the New World by degrees transforms the economic life of the Old. With Adam Smith and Karl Marx as its patron saints, this doctrine could look forward to a friendly reception in the twentieth-century world. It was duly reformulated in modern terminology by Professor Earl J. Hamilton in a famous essay, 'American Treasure and the Rise of Capitalism'.[3] This essay examined various encouragements to the growth of capitalism in sixteenth-century Europe—the rise of nation-states, the demands of war, the rise of Protestantism—

---

[1] *Wealth of Nations*, bk. iv, c. vii, pt. iii (ed. Cannan, London, 1961, ii, 141–2).
[2] Karl Marx and Friedrich Engels, 'The Communist Manifesto', *Selected Works* (2 vols. Moscow, 1951), i, 34.
[3] *Economica*, ix (1929), 338–57.

and concluded that the discovery of America was the principal stimulus to European capital formation. The consequence of the discovery was to encourage the growth of European industries, which had to supply manufactures in exchange for the produce of America; to provide Europe with the silver which it required for its trade with the East—a trade which contributed powerfully to capital formation because of the vast profits which accrued to its promoters; and to provoke a price revolution in Europe, which again facilitated capital accumulation because wages lagged behind prices.

Hamilton's essay belonged to the great debate about the rise of capitalism—a debate which testifies to a continuing preoccupation with the reasons for Europe's domination of the world. Why did Europe launch out at the end of the Middle Ages on its unique historical course, as a civilization which would dedicate itself to economic growth, technological advance and world-wide expansion? One possibility is that the answer is intrinsic to Europe itself—that it lies in certain special features of European civilization, as it emerged in the Early Modern period. The two most favoured candidates have been the Protestant Reformation and that rather vague phenomenon which wanders through European historical writing under the title of 'Renaissance individualism'. But there is an alternative possibility—that the answer, to a greater or lesser degree, is extrinsic to Europe; that some external agency started Europe on its road to success, and helped to sustain it whenever its steps began to falter. Here the outstanding candidate is America.

The balance of Hamilton's argument came down on the side of extrinsic causes, and his later work tended to narrow the range of his 1929 article by concentrating on one particular aspect of America's contribution to the growth of European capitalism—the supply of gold and silver. This monetarist explanation of European economic growth has come in for some hard words in recent years, but it is by no means dead and buried; or, if dead, it has been triumphantly resurrected, and indeed rejuvenated, by M. Pierre Chaunu. By widening the discussion from the bullion supply to embrace the whole scope of the transatlantic trade, M. Chaunu has given new life and vigour to the American explanation of Europe's economic expansion.[1]

Hamilton and Chaunu tended to confine themselves to the more technical aspects of America's contribution to Europe's economic development, and remained firmly committed to the world of price and trade statistics. But eighteenth-century authors were prepared to range widely over the question of America's general influence on Europe's morals, government and opinions; and this approach has also found some favour in the present century. In a chapter on the influence of the discoveries, in his *Aspects of the Rise of Economic Individualism*, Mr H. M. Robertson argued that the importance of the discoveries 'is not confined to the strictly material sphere. For the consequent expansion of commerce meant a necessary expansion of ideas.' The essence of his argument was that the discoveries meant 'an increase of opportunity'; that 'business methods changed with the enlargement of the economic horizon'; and that from these new opportunities there emerged an entrepreneurial class with a spirit of capitalism and of economic individualism, which acted as a solvent on traditional society.[2]

Robertson's argument was only part of a much more wide-ranging critique of the theory which would link capitalism with the rise of Protestantism, and it was left to a Texan historian, Walter Prescott Webb, to bring the New World to the centre of the stage, by developing a thesis which goes far beyond the merely 'material' consequences of the discovery of America to provide a comprehensive interpretation of modern history in terms of the New World and its impact on Europe.

The 'American' interpretation of European history offered by Webb in *The Great Frontier*[3] is, admittedly, comprehensive rather than total. Obeisance is made, in passing, both to the Renaissance and to Luther, although not, rather strangely, to Calvin. The Renaissance is described as delivering the mind, and Luther as delivering the spirit, of European man. To this extent at least, then, Webb accepted the hypothesis that certain developments within European civilization itself formed the prelude to the new historical

---

[1] H. and P. Chaunu, *Séville et l'Atlantique* (8 vols. Paris, 1955–9).
[2] (Cambridge, 1933), pp. 176 and 177.   [3] (London, 1953).

57

epoch. But Columbus, he continued, 'delivered the body by providing a substance and setting for the three freedoms'.[1] In linking Columbus and Luther, Webb—whether consciously or unconsciously—was in fact echoing a passage written by the Abbé Raynal: 'Luther and Columbus appeared; the whole universe trembled, and all Europe was in commotion . . . One of these persons awakened the understandings of all men, the other excited their activity.'[2] But Webb went much further than any of his predecessors in making Columbus's achievement central to European development. He did this by appropriating the frontier thesis originally advanced by Frederick Jackson Turner to explain the course of American history, and applying it instead to the history of Europe.

According to Webb's argument, Europe should be regarded as the metropolis, and America as its Great Frontier. The opening of this Great Frontier by Columbus transformed the prospects for Europe in that it decisively altered the ratio between the three factors of population, land and capital in such a way as to create boom conditions. In 1500 Europe's 3,750,000 square miles of land were occupied by a population of some 100 million, giving a density of 26·7 persons to the square mile. With the discovery of America—the opening of the Great Frontier—these 100 million people acquired an additional twenty million square miles of land, with all the subsequent possibilities of a dramatically reduced density of settlement. As a result of the exploitation of the New World, the relatively stable population of Europe now found itself suddenly presented with a surplus of land and capital; and the dramatic alteration of the ratio between land, people and capital launched Europe on four centuries of boom, which came to an end with the closing of the frontier around the year 1900.

The period 1500–1900 is therefore presented by Webb as a unique period in history—the period in which the Great Frontier of America shapes and transforms Western civilization. With the courage (and also the genius for oversimplification) of the Texan, he then set out to trace the impact of the American frontier as a modifier of European institutions, the European economy and European thought. This was an epic undertaking, requiring a far

[1] P. 104.　　　　　　　　　　[2] *A Philosophical and Political History*, iv, 401.

greater knowledge of European history than Webb himself possessed;
and inevitably it left him wide open to criticism on a large number of
fronts. But it remains the first serious attempt since the eighteenth
century to assess European history in terms of the impact of America.
As such, it deserves two cheers for gallantry, although not—regret-
tably—three cheers for success.[1]

In so far as Webb was concerned with the economic impact of
America, he followed in the steps of Adam Smith and Earl J.
Hamilton, although he adopted a Frontier terminology in describing
the material benefits of America as 'windfalls' for Europe. Native
American produce and precious metals were the primary windfalls,
which gave an immediate impetus to sixteenth- and seventeenth-
century European capitalism, while the long-term development
of American resources created secondary windfalls, which helped to
sustain that capitalism in the eighteenth and nineteenth centuries.
But he also concerned himself with those non-material benefits
briefly discussed by H. M. Robertson. These benefits can be
summarized in his phrase 'modern dynamism', whose genesis he
discovered in the frontier setting of European history since the age
of Columbus.

In Webb's *Great Frontier*, therefore, is to be found an extended,
if in some respects idiosyncratic, résumé of most of the traditional
arguments about the economic impact of America on Europe. If we
look at those arguments, we find that they all tend to be variations
on three recurrent themes—the stimulating effects of bullion, trade,
and opportunity. It is therefore worth examining each of these three
themes, to see how far the information that is available about them
can bear the weight of interpretation that has been placed upon it.

'How much the richest empire in the world is that of these Indies',
wrote Fernández de Oviedo in one of his periodic moments of
lyrical effusion about the wealth of the newly-discovered lands.[2]
This wealth was by no means confined to precious metals. Sixteenth-
century Europe obtained from America considerable quantities of

---

[1] For criticisms of the Webb thesis, see in particular part iv of *The New World Looks at
its History*, ed. A. R. Lewis and T. F. McGann (Austin, Texas, 1963), and the generally
favourable, but by no means uncritical, assessment by Geoffrey Barraclough in c. x of
his *History in a Changing World* (Oxford, 1955).   [2] *Historia General*, i, 156.

pearls and emeralds, together with more utilitarian products—foods and dyestuffs—which constituted, in Webb's language, an important 'windfall', in the sense that Europe's general stock was augmented by products which were either unknown, or which had previously been in short supply. But inevitably it was the gold and silver of the New World which most attracted the attention of sixteenth-century Europeans. 'Those lands do not produce bread or wine', wrote Pérez de Oliva in the 1520s, 'but they do produce large quantities of gold, in which lordship consists.'[1]

Gold was power. This had always been the Castilian attitude to wealth,[2] and the discovery of gold in the Indies seemed to fulfil an old Castilian dream. But the finding of gold, and, still more, of silver, also fulfilled a genuine European need. Medieval Europe did not exist in a monetary vacuum. On the contrary, its stocks of gold and silver rose and fell in response to global movements over which it exercised little control. When the Moslem world was minting gold coins, as it was between AD. 1000 and the mid-thirteenth century, Christendom was minting silver; and when, in the later Middle Ages, the silver famine of the Moslem world was eased, and its silver currencies began to replace gold, Europe started minting large numbers of gold coins, while its silver reserves ran increasingly low. In this intricate counterpoint of Europe and Asia, Europe seems to have been relatively well endowed with gold in the late fifteenth century, but the Mediterranean regions in particular were acutely short of silver.[3]

The influx of a stream of American bullion into Europe needs to be set into this global context—a context in which different rates between gold and silver in Europe and Asia caused large-scale flows of both metals in opposite directions. Between 1500 and 1650 something like 181 tons of gold and 16,000 tons of silver reached Europe officially from America,[4] and further large quantities must have arrived by contraband. Attempts to relate these figures to those for the existing stocks of precious metals in Europe have not proved very

---

[1] Fernando Pérez de Oliva, *Las Obras* (Córdoba, 1586), f. 135 v.
[2] See Pedro Corominas, *El Sentimiento de la Riqueza en Castilla* (Madrid, 1917).
[3] See Andrew M. Watson, 'Back to Gold—and Silver', *Economic History Review*, 2nd series, xx (1967), 1–34.
[4] *The Cambridge Economic History of Europe*, iv (Cambridge, 1967), 445.

successful; but one could reasonably expect that the influx of such a large quantity of precious metals would have considerable consequences, not only for Europe's monetary system, but also for the character of its economic relationship with the outer world.

The first bullion imports from America were gold imports, and it was only in the decade 1531–40 that silver secured its dramatic lead.[1] In the opening decades of the sixteenth century, therefore, more gold was coming to a Europe already relatively well supplied with gold; and if there was any casualty, it was the gold of the Sahara, which had helped to sustain the economic life of Europe in the later Middle Ages.[2] It was only in the second half of the sixteenth century that American silver production, outpacing that of the Tyrolese mines, began to satisfy a Europe which had been silver-hungry for so long. One consequence of the new availability of silver was to push up the price of gold relative to that of silver—by the early seventeenth century the ratio of gold to silver exceeded one to twelve.[3] A further consequence was to enable Europeans to acquire larger quantities of those Far Eastern luxuries for which Asia insisted on silver in exchange. Unfortunately, it is impossible to know with any certainty what proportion of Europe's American silver flowed out again to the East during the great silver-age of the sixteenth century. In the seventeenth century there came a moment when Asia was glutted with silver from the American mines.[4] But, at least until that moment, the windfall of American silver enabled Europe to buy oriental goods which it could not otherwise have afforded, to the consequent benefit of a European élite which hankered after exotic luxuries, and of those members of the merchant community who were able to supply them.

If the bullion of the New World helped to change the economic relationship of Europe to Asia, how far did it also stimulate economic and social change inside Europe itself? The arguments traditionally advanced are that the influx of American silver provoked a revolu-

[1] Earl J. Hamilton, *American Treasure and the Price Revolution in Spain, 1501–1650* (Cambridge, Mass., 1934), pp. 40–2.
[2] Frank C. Spooner, *L'Economie Mondiale et les Frappes Monétaires en France, 1493–1680* (Paris, 1956), pp. 10–13.
[3] *Cambridge Economic History of Europe*, iv, 385 (and figure 5, p. 459).
[4] Spooner, *L'Economie Mondiale*, pp. 71–2.

tion in prices, which began in Spain and then spread by degrees to other parts of the continent; that this price revolution inflated the profits of merchants and manufacturers as prices forged ahead of costs and wages, and consequently encouraged both capital formation and industrial growth; and that the inflationary conditions created rapid social change, because influential sections of society, living on relatively fixed incomes, found themselves at a disadvantage compared with those social groups which were dynamic enough, or sufficiently well placed, to seize the opportunities offered them by rising price levels.

All these arguments raise complex questions, which still seem to be waiting for satisfactory answers. Whether or not the financial history of sixteenth-century Europe justifies so emotive a description as 'price revolution', the fact remains that a society which had grown used to relative price stability was faced over the course of the sixteenth-century with a fivefold rise in prices, and that this novel phenomenon caused it much bewilderment and concern. If their search for its causes led contemporaries in due course to American silver, this was in line with a well-established scholastic tradition which related the level of prices to the scarcity or abundance of precious metals.[1] This tradition was amply confirmed by the experiences of the conquerors and colonists in the New World itself. López de Gómara, who is sometimes given credit for his early perception of the relationship between American silver and Spanish price levels on the strength of a remark in his manuscript *Annals of the Emperor Charles V*,[2] did in fact note in his published *History of the Indies* that, as a consequence of the distribution of Atahualpa's treasure among the conquerors of Peru, 'the price of things grew dear with the amount of money there was'.[3] Reports of this kind, spread by the *conquistadores* themselves, and reproduced in histories of the conquest, would certainly have helped to popularize, in Spain and outside it, the idea that a close correlation existed between the amount of silver in circulation and the general level of prices.

Twelve years before Bodin's famous exposition in 1568 of the

---

[1] Marjorie Grice-Hutchinson, *The School of Salamanca* (Oxford, 1952), p. 52; Pierre Vilar, *Crecimiento y Desarollo* (Barcelona, 1964), pp. 181–2.
[2] Hamilton, *American Treasure*, p. 292.
[3] *Historia General de las Indias* (1552), p. 231.

causes of the price rise,[1] Martín de Azpilcueta Navarro, of the School of Salamanca, had clearly related the high cost of living in Spain to the influx of American silver.[2] It was twenty years since Fernández de Oviedo had written that Spain was one of the richest provinces in the world, and that God had chosen to bestow upon it the crowning glory of the additional riches of the Indies.[3] When Oviedo wrote these words, the Castilian economy had been enjoying the benefits of a rapidly growing market across the Atlantic. But when Azpilcueta wrote, the economic climate was already beginning to change. The prices of Castilian goods were rising faster than those of other countries, and Castile's balance of trade with other parts of Europe was worsening, as it imported more from them, exported less to them, and bridged the gap with American silver. This gradual change in economic circumstances was accompanied by a growing disillusionment with the riches of America, which was reflected in the mounting volume of complaints from the Cortes of Castile about the rise in prices, and in a growing profusion of comments about the morally harmful effects of wealth.[4] Castile's very success was the source of its undoing. 'Novus orbis victus vos vicit'—'the New World, conquered by you, has conquered you in its turn'—wrote Justus Lipsius to a Spanish friend in 1603.[5]

But what exactly had brought about this defeat? Was it the outcome of a purely technical process—the flooding of Spain with precious metals, which had raised its price levels sharply above those of other European states? Was it, as the Castilian Cortes suggested in the middle years of the century, the result of an excessive diversion of home-produced commodities to the American export-market, and the consequent creation of scarcity and high costs at home? Or was this essentially a moral and psychological problem—the result of a misappropriation of wealth, nurtured on a lust for riches that was too

[1] *La Response de Jean Bodin à M. de Malestroit*, ed. Henri Hauser (Paris, 1932), pp. 9–10. It is noteworthy that Bodin uses the experience of the Spaniards in America to support his argument that it is 'l'abondance qui cause le mespris'.
[2] The relevant passage is to be found, in translation, on p. 95 of Grice-Hutchinson, *The School of Salamanca*.
[3] *Historia General*, i, 163
[4] F. Morales Padrón, 'L'Amérique dans la Littérature Espagnole', *La Découverte de l'Amérique*, pp. 285–6.
[5] Alejandro Ramírez, *Epistolario de Justo Lipsio y los Españoles* (Madrid, 1966), p. 372.

easily satisfied? Some people, wrote Garcilaso de la Vega around 1612, 'say that this flood of riches has done more harm than good, since wealth commonly produces vice rather than virtue, inclining its possessors to pride, ambition, gluttony and voluptuousness . . . The conclusion is that the riches of the New World, properly understood, have not increased the volume of useful things necessary for human life, such as food and clothing, but have made them scarcer and rendered men effeminate in their power of understanding and in their bodies, dress, and customs, and that they lived more happily and were more feared by the rest of the world with what they had formerly.'[1]

These various contemporary attempts at explanation were not necessarily mutually incompatible. All of them could draw on long-established traditions about commodities and prices and the social and moral consequences of excessive riches, and all of them could to some extent be verified by empirical observation. In placing his own emphasis on the first of these interpretations—the purely monetary explanation—Professor Hamilton was pursuing a theme which had a special attraction in the economic circumstances of the 1920s and 1930s. But the difficulties in the way of accepting an essentially monetary interpretation, either of Spanish or of European price-movements, are formidable, and they have not diminished with the years. There is no need to rehearse yet again the various objections that have been raised against Hamilton's explanation of the price rise in Spain,[2] but it is impossible to avoid all mention of the difficulties inherent in his central argument that a close correlation has been established between the movement of Spanish commodity prices and the arrival of fresh silver remittances in Seville.

The fate of American silver once it reached Seville remains almost as much of a mystery now as when Hamilton wrote, but it is precisely on this question of its destination that his argument finally

[1] *Royal Commentaries* (trans. Livermore), part ii (*The Conquest of Peru*), pp. 647–8.
[2] See especially J. Nadal Oller, 'La Revolución de los Precios Españoles en el Siglo XVI', *Hispania*, xix (1959), 503–29; also, J. H. Elliott, *Imperial Spain, 1469–1716* (London, 1963), pp. 183–8, for a general summary. The most cogent general discussion of the problem of the price revolution remains I. Hammarström, 'The "Price Revolution" of the Sixteenth Century: Some Swedish Evidence', *Scandinavian Economic History Review*, v (1957), 118–54.

turns. How much of the silver reaching Seville really entered the Spanish monetary system? One would hardly expect the proportion to remain constant in relation to the remittances from America, if only because the despatch of silver to other parts of Europe was bound to vary according to the foreign policy commitments of the Spanish Crown, and according to the capacity of Spain itself to meet its own needs and those of the American market without recourse to foreign goods that had to be paid for—at least in part—with silver. An official estimate of 1594 indicates that, out of an average annual remittance from the Indies of some ten million ducats, six million were leaving Spain each year—three million to meet the foreign expenses of the Crown, and three million to the account of private individuals. Instead of ten million ducats being injected into the Spanish monetary system, therefore, the figure is only four million, at the very most.[1]

The distribution of those precious metals which remained in Spain—itself divided up into different regional economies—is again a matter of great uncertainty. For the years 1570 and 1571, however, the dispersion of precious metals through the peninsula has been traced; and in these years, at least, the highest proportion went to Valladolid, followed by Seville and Cadiz, and then Madrid.[2] The attraction of Valladolid lay primarily in its proximity to the international fairs of Medina del Campo, but it was also an important centre for silver and gold work. With its judges and officials, and its resident nobles and merchants, Valladolid boasted an affluent patrician class, and the inventories of its citizens' wealth reveal the presence of many objects of silver and gold in their houses.[3] It would certainly be reasonable to expect that a proportion of the bullion entering the peninsula—and perhaps even a significant proportion—was not converted to monetary uses, but was transformed into objects of fine workmanship for the greater glory of God and man. How far, indeed, would Baroque art, as an art heavily dependent on gold and silver ornamentation, have been possible without the riches of the Indies?

[1] F. Ruiz Martín, *Lettres Marchandes Echangées entre Florence et Medina del Campo* (Paris, 1965), p. xlix.
[2] José Gentil Da Silva, *En Espagne* (Paris, 1965), pp. 67 ff.
[3] Bartolomé Bennassar, *Valladolid au Siècle d'Or* (Paris, 1967), p. 459.

Moving outwards from Spain to other parts of Europe, similar difficulties arise in any attempt to correlate the influx of silver and the movement of prices. The various causes of the seepage of silver from Spain are well enough known in general terms, but the process cannot yet be reconstructed with any precision of detail. Government spending abroad, on armies and embassies and subsidies to allies; divergent bimetallic ratios and an adverse balance of trade; smuggling, and the legal export of specie through special licences, which began to be granted with considerable prodigality from the mid-1560s[1]—all this helped to distribute the riches of the Indies through the continent.[2] But it is not easy to establish any clear cause-and-effect relationship between movements of American silver and price rises in England, for example, or in Italy.[3]

The explanation of the sixteenth-century price revolution in terms of American silver, therefore, obviously leaves some major unresolved problems. It would be desirable to know what proportion of the silver disappeared into the remoteness of Asia, and what proportion of the silver which actually remained in Europe was used for non-monetary purposes. Most of all, it would be desirable to know, both for Spain and for Europe as a whole, the degree of responsibility to be allotted to American bullion in forcing up prices, as against other monetary causes—such as changes in the bimetallic ratio, debasements, and inflationary fiscal policies—and as against 'real' causes, like poor harvests, or (today's most favoured candidate) population pressure.

The final conclusion may well be that the presence of American silver helped to maintain prices at a generally high level, even if it did not necessarily act as the original stimulus to upward movements of prices. It still remains necessary, however, to consider the validity of certain assumptions about the *consequences* of inflationary conditions in the sixteenth century. Hamilton argued that capitalism was stimulated by the lag between wages and prices, and that this

[1] Ruiz Martín, *Lettres Marchandes*, p. xxxviii.
[2] The map by Alvaro Castillo, reproduced on p. 463 of *The Cambridge Economic History of Europe*, vol. iv, gives a good general idea of the distribution of American silver through Europe.
[3] For England, see the helpful pamphlet by R. B. Outhwaite, *Inflation in Tudor and Early Stuart England* (London, 1969); for Italy, C. M. Cipolla, 'La Prétendue Révolution des Prix', *Annales*, x (1955), 513–16.

lag inflated the profits of entrepreneurs. But the evidence for an inflation of industrial profits remains unconvincing.[1] This argument, however, is in effect only one part, and not the most important part, of the more general thesis which would link capital formation and the rise of the bourgeoisie to the financial benefits accruing from the exploitation of the Indies. Vast profits could certainly be gained from intelligent entrepreneurship in America. After eight years in Panama, Gaspar de Espinosa is alleged to have returned home to Spain in 1522 with the enormous fortune of a million gold *pesos*.[2] But what did the successful do with their profits from the Indies? Some of the money was reinvested in further commercial or financial enterprises, at home or in America; some of it was used to grease the palms of royal officials; some of it was gambled away. But much of it was inevitably devoted to improving the status of merchant families and enabling them to live in the manner of the aristocracy. A study of the great Espinosa dynasty in sixteenth-century Spain records sixty-nine members of the family as business-men. Of these, forty-four had commercial contacts with the Indies.[3] Many of them look and behave like Sombart's archetypal capitalists; but the final impression given by the Espinosa family history is of a gradual retreat from business, and of the transformation of entrepreneurs into comfortable *rentiers*.

It may well be that, for various local reasons, this process was unusally frequent, and unusually serious in its consequences, in sixteenth-century Castile. But what Braudel has called 'la trahison de la bourgeoisie'[4] was a phenomenon which knew no frontiers in sixteenth-century Europe, and it would be difficult to show that European society at the end of the century was any more distinctively 'bourgeois' in outlook than at the beginning of it. Rising prices and enhanced opportunities for profit sharpened the inequalities which already existed within European society. But the price revolution of the sixteenth century did not alter the social

[1] J. U. Nef, 'Prices and Industrial Capitalism in France and England, 1540–1640', *EconomicHistory Review*, vii (1937), 155–85; D. Felix, 'Profit Inflation and Industrial Growth', *Quarterly Journal of Economics*, lxx (1956), 441–63.
[2] Guillermo Lohmann Villena, *Les Espinosa* (Paris, 1968), p. 167.
[3] *Ibid.* p. 131.
[4] Fernand Braudel, *La Méditerranée et le Monde Méditerranéen à l'époque de Philippe II* (Paris, 1949), p. 619.

framework itself. Great nobles became heavily indebted, but many of them learnt to live happily enough with their debts in an age of easy credit. Merchants, business-men, lawyers and royal officials made their fortunes, settled their families, and aped the habits of the nobles. American silver, acquired at first or second hand, may have eased the entry of new families into the privileged ranks of society, but those ranks closed again around them, without any marked alteration in their accustomed mode of life.

It would seem legitimate, therefore, to entertain some doubts about the role of American silver as the prime source of dynamic change in sixteenth-century Europe. But may there not be a better candidate than American silver—the American trade itself? Europe urgently needed the silver of the Indies, partly to acquire oriental products, and partly to satisfy the needs of its own increased economic activity. But some of this increase in economic activity was itself the direct result of the opening up of a new and expanding American market, which came to expect a growing quantity, and a growing variety, of European commodities. America's needs therefore stimulated the growth of European industries, from ship-building to textiles, and the economic growth of sixteenth-century Europe became closely tied to the expansion of the Spanish-Atlantic trade.

This is the central thesis propounded by M. and Mme. Chaunu, who have launched upon the historical ocean a mighty flotilla of volumes, heavily freighted with hypotheses, statistics and facts. They have provided us with a monumental list of the names and tonnage of the ships which made the Atlantic crossing between Seville and the Indies over a century and a half; they have established in the most meticulous detail the actual mechanism of Seville's transatlantic trade; and they have worked out a pattern for this trade which suggests a close correlation with the movement of prices in Amsterdam, and hence with the wider movements of the European economy.[1]

The general nature of this pattern is by now well known. The years 1504–50 are depicted as the first great age of European ex-

---

[1] *Séville et l'Atlantique*. Volumes VIII (i), VIII (ii,i) and VIII (ii,ii) constitute the 'partie interprétative' of this formidable work.

pansion—the age of the moving frontier in America; of conquest, colonization and the first influx of bullion, which stimulates investment at home. There follows a twelve-year hiatus, when the conquests are complete and the systematic exploitation of the resources of the Indies has yet to get under way. But after 1562, the colonial demand for European goods is intensified; there is a rapid increase in the output of silver which will pay for these goods; and the Seville trade expands. As more treasure flows into Seville, more becomes available both for the Spanish Crown and for European entrepreneurs, but at the same time more of it has to be invested in the ships and the cargoes of the expanding Atlantic trade. It appears that around 1570, for instance, about half the sum which arrived from the Indies in bullion each year was being employed to freight the fleets for their next transatlantic voyage.[1] Finally, at the beginning of the seventeenth century, saturation-point is reached. The colonial market for European goods has reached the limits of its expansion; and from about 1622, with the American demand falling off, silver reaches Seville in diminishing quantities, Seville's Atlantic trade slumps decisively both in value and volume, and Europe enters its depression of the mid-seventeenth century.

There is an elegance and a simplicity about this explanation of European economic fluctuations in terms of the trade of Seville which makes the Chaunu thesis immediately attractive. Just as the expansion of the eighteenth-century economy might be linked to the development of the colonial empires of the northern nations, so the earlier expansion of sixteenth-century Europe might be linked to the development of Spain's colonial empire.[2] Between these two great ages of expansion lies the seventeenth-century depression. Such an argument would be neat; but neat arguments should properly arouse the suspicions of the historian, whose explorations of the past ought to have made him aware of the untidiness of life. Apart from any problems about the character and completeness of the documentation used by the Chaunus, and the regrettable absence of information about the contents of the cargoes,[3] there remains the crucial question of

[1] Da Silva, *En Espagne*, p. 65.
[2] See the review by H. G. Koenigsberger, *English Historical Review*, 76 (1961), 675–81.
[3] See the reviews by Enrique Otte, *Moneda y Crédito*, no. 80 (1962), 137–41, and W. Brulez, *Revue Belge de Philologie et d'Histoire*, xlii (1964), 568–92.

the Atlantic trade relative to other branches of European commerce.

Are there, in particular, overwhelming reasons for assuming that the fluctuations of the Spanish-Atlantic trading system affected the European economy more profoundly than the fluctuations of the Baltic trade, which exceeded the Seville trade in volume?[1] If there are, these are likely to arise from the contribution made by the Atlantic trade to Europe's stock of precious metals. This leads back to an essentially monetarist interpretation of European economic expansion, which would relate the growth or stagnation of Europe's economy to the output of the American mines, and to the quantities of American bullion reaching Europe.

It is perfectly possible to construct an explanation of Europe's 'seventeenth-century depression' (if indeed such a phenomenon occurred) in terms of changing conditions on the far side of the Atlantic. These changing conditions could be the consequence of growing economic self-sufficiency in the Spanish Indies, as the colonists came to produce for themselves many of the commodities which they had previously imported from Europe. This would have brought about a decline in the shipment of cargoes from Seville, and a resulting decline in the amount of silver remitted to Europe to pay for them. Alternatively, there could be a switch in the deployment of American silver, related to changing needs in the Indies. More could be held back by the viceroys for administrative and military purposes, and more could have found its way directly to Asia by way of the Pacific, as the colonists developed a taste for oriental luxuries. A further possibility, which has found considerable favour, is that the decline of silver remittances to Seville reflects growing difficulties in the mining economies of Mexico and Peru. There came a time when the easier veins of silver were exhausted, and the technical problems involved in extracting the metal multiplied. There were mounting problems, too, connected with the production and supply of mercury, on which the silver-refining process depended. Above all, there was the catastrophic decline in the native Indian population, which

[1] A. P. Usher, 'Spanish Ships and Shipping in the Sixteenth and Seventeenth Centuries', *Facts and Factors in Economic History. Articles by Former Students of E. F. Gay* (Cambridge, Mass. 1932), p. 210. See also Pierre Jeannin, 'Les Comptes du Sund comme Source pour la Construction d'Indices Généraux de l'Activité Economique en Europe', *Revue Historique*, 231 (1964), 55–102, 307–40.

affected the labour supply, and undermined the traditional base of the Spanish colonial economy.

These various possibilities are by no means mutually exclusive, and between them they create a composite picture of conditions in the Indies which carries more conviction than would a mono-causal explanation of change. But even if it is agreed that Mexico and Peru underwent profound changes between the later sixteenth and mid-seventeenth centuries—changes which for one reason or another made them less dependent on their European life-line—there still remains the problem of the degree to which these changes in the Indies should be held accountable for Europe's troubles.[1]

It would, for instance, be perfectly possible to construct a quite different, and perhaps equally plausible, model of the relationship between Europe and America, in which the emphasis would be placed on changing needs and circumstances in Europe, rather than the Indies. In this alternative model, considerable attention would have to be paid (as it is indeed paid by Chaunu himself) to the fiscal policies of the Spanish Crown. Struggling to pay its armies and sustain its prodigious military effort, it increasingly resorted to the confiscation of silver remittances reaching Seville for private individuals. The effect of repeated sequestrations was inevitably to introduce a high degree of insecurity into Seville's trade, and to deter European merchants from despatching cargoes, and their agents in the Indies from sending back silver to Europe.

But there is also a wider possible explanation, which relates to monetary conditions and the general state of economic activity in seventeenth-century Europe. May it not be that Europe in the seventeenth century had less need of American silver than it had in the sixteenth century? A study of the Zacatecas silver mines shows the need to set the history of the mines in the seventeenth century against the background of a European economy in which the value of silver in terms of gold was falling.[2] With gold becoming scarcer and silver

---

[1] On the basis of the work of Chaunu, Borah and others, John Lynch provides in vol. ii of his *Spain Under the Habsburgs* (Oxford, 1969) an account of seventeenth-century Spanish history which places a heavy emphasis on changing conditions in Spain's American colonies as a cause of depression at home.

[2] P. J. Bakewell, *Silver Mining and Society in Zacatecas, 1550–1700* (unpublished Cambridge Ph.D. thesis, 1969, deposited in the Cambridge University Library). I am very grateful to Dr Bakewell for allowing me to make use of his thesis in this context.

more common, Europeans were not willing to pay so much for their silver, and the mining communities of the New World inevitably felt the consequences. A decline in European demand at remunerative rates of payment may therefore have led to a decline in the output of the American mines. But this decline in demand need not be exclusively related to changes in the gold–silver ratio. It might equally well be connected with an extension of, and improvement in, European credit facilities. It might also be related to a general slowing-down of Europe's economic growth after the feverish activity of the sixteenth century—a process which could be explained by any number of circumstances: poor harvests, the devastations of war, the end of the great population increase.

This particular model would once more make conditions intrinsic to Europe the prime source of economic and social change. But this, too, seems unsatisfactory, in view of the agonizing dependence of sixteenth-century Europe's financial machinery on the safe and regular arrival of the treasure-fleet at Seville. A delayed arrival was reason for acute anxiety in the courts and counting-houses of Europe; and the world of international finance breathed more easily as reports arrived that the galleons were dropping anchor at San Lúcar. It was precisely because a close reciprocal relationship had been established in the sixteenth century, that neither the Old World nor the New could any longer expect to live in isolation by the seventeenth. Inevitably each acted upon, and reacted to, the other. But a significant change does appear to have come over their mutual relationship in the opening decades of the seventeenth century. Neither now needed, as much as it needed in the past, what the other had to offer. There was a diminishing demand in the Indies for European goods, and a diminishing demand in Europe for American silver. As a result, their economies failed to complement each other as neatly as they had in earlier years; and when each ran into difficulties, neither could offer at this moment the exact form of assistance which would have relieved the other's troubles.

This suggests that any definition of the relationship between Europe and America in terms of either silver or trade is not in itself enough. There must also have been a question of opportunity.

If the exploitation of the New World's resources in the sixteenth century acted as a stimulus to economic activity in Europe, this indicates a fortunate conjunction of favourable circumstances and of men with the willingness, the initiative and the capacity to make the most of them. It is here that Webb's thesis of the 'Great Frontier' may be able to contribute something of value, for the outstanding characteristic of the Great Frontier was that it 'offered an unlimited outlet for enterprise and investment'.[1] Might it, then, be said that the discovery of the New World created an awareness of new economic opportunities, which itself provided a stimulus to change?

One of the earliest and most unequivocal appreciations of the economic opportunities created by the discovery of America is to be found in a memorandum addressed to the city fathers of Córdoba by the humanist Hernán Pérez de Oliva in 1524.[2] He rebuked the city council for its neglect of the river Guadalquivir, which gave it access to the sea. It was, he argued, even more important now than in the past to improve navigation along this great waterway, 'because formerly we were at the end of the world, and now we are in the middle of it, with an unprecedented change in our fortunes'. As a believer in the westward movement of empires, he saw the seat of world power coming to rest in Spain. 'Well then, gentlemen, take advantage of the great fortune that is now coming to Spain. Make your river navigable, and you will have opened for yourselves a road by which you can participate in this fortune, and bring to your families great prosperity.' Instead of its ancient rival, Seville, reaping all the advantages, these would now accrue to Córdoba, which would supply the inhabitants of the Indies with the goods they required, and would receive the gold of the Indies in payment. 'From these isles of the west will come so many ships laden with wealth, and so many will sail to them, that I believe they will leave a permanent imprint on the waters of the sea.'

Pérez de Oliva was perhaps unusual in his capacity to envisage, both for his country and his native city, the great new opportunities which had been created by the discovery of America. He already saw in his mind's eye impressive new buildings rising in Córdoba—a

[1] *The Great Frontier*, p. 417.   [2] *Obras*, fs. 129 v–139 v.

university, a chancellery, a merchants' exchange, a mint. Unfortunately, the city authorities of Córdoba did not show themselves equal to the grandiose vision of the prophet in their midst. But elsewhere, especially in Seville, men not only glimpsed the new horizons, but also showed themselves ready to translate visions into deeds.

In the first years after the discovery, there may well have been doubts, particularly in official circles. José Pellicer, writing in 1640, claims that some people argued that it was a mistake for Spaniards to become involved in the discovery and colonization of the Indies, and that kingdoms grew rich on the skill and enterprise of their inhabitants, and not on the working of distant silver-mines.[1] But, in the event, the financial necessities of the Spanish Crown and the desire for private gain combined to produce a massive investment of men, money and enterprise in the development of the Indies.

This process was both facilitated and stimulated by the commercial outlook and expertise of important groups in the city of Seville at the time of America's discovery. Here was a city with a rich hinterland, and relatively easy access to the sea, which had already established itself as a great international port and trading-centre, and had attracted considerable numbers of foreign merchants, including a powerful colony of Genoese. In this cosmopolitan atmosphere it would be natural to expect a degree of openness to new ideas, and a sharp eye for profit. The Canaries, the West Indies and the mainland of America, in turn, seemed to offer promising enough opportunities for profitable investment to tempt even those sections of society which were not professionally dedicated to commercial enterprise. Tomás de Mercado, writing in the 1560s, described how the discovery of the Indies, some sixty years earlier, had created an opportunity for the acquisition of great wealth, and had 'attracted some of the principal citizens into becoming merchants, when they saw the vast profits to be gained'. The result was a new social mobility, 'for the gentry, through greed or necessity have lowered themselves, if not to trade, at least to inter-marry with trading families; and the merchants, with their desire for nobility, have striven to rise, and establish rich entailed estates'.[2]

[1] *Comercio Impedido* (printed memorandum, dated 30 January 1640) p.2 v. (Catalogued in British Museum under *Comercio*, but not under the name of Pellicer.)
[2] *Summa de Tratos*, p. 15–15 v.

The new frontier

If one consequence of the discovery and development of the Indies was to create a greater *social* mobility in the city of Seville, another was to promote still greater *geographical* mobility among a population which had for centuries shown strong nomadic tendencies. Inevitably the new prosperity of Seville attracted merchants from outside, like the Espinosa family, who moved from Medina de Rioseco in the early sixteenth century in order to participate at first hand in the lucrative commercial ventures that beckoned in the Indies.[1] Although the Genoese merchant community made a valuable contribution to the development of the Indies,[2] it is doubtful whether this contribution can compare with that of native Spaniards—Andalusians, Basques, Burgaleses—who had seen Seville's new possibilities as the capital of a transatlantic world.[3] These men had realized that Europe's frontier had moved, and that this move in turn had brought a shift in the centre of economic gravity. Pérez de Oliva had said as much in his address to the city councillors of Córdoba, and the same theme was repeated by Tomás de Mercado, as he expatiated on the prosperity of Seville. 'Previously, Andalusia and Lusitania used to be the very end of the world, but now, with the discovery of the Indies, they have become its centre.'[4]

But it was not only the merchants who felt the lure of Seville. It acted as a magnet for the population of Castile—for the restless, the ambitious and the hungry, who drifted southwards in the hope of sharing, at least at second-hand, in the prosperity brought by the Indies. The splendours and miseries of the teeming streets of Seville—a city with a population of 100,000 or more by the end of the sixteenth century—provided the most striking visual evidence anywhere in Europe of the impact of America on sixteenth-century life.[5]

Many of those who arrived in Seville made it the end of their

---

1 Lohmann Villena, *Les Espinosa*, p. 15.

2 Ruth Pike, *Enterprise and Adventure* (Ithaca, New York, 1966).

3 Enrique Otte, 'Das Genuesische Unternehmertum und Amerika unter den Katholischen Königen', *Jahrbuch für Geschichte von Staat, Wirtschaft und Gesellschaft Lateinamerikas*, ii (1965), 30–74.

4 *Summa de Tratos*, p. 15 v.

5 Antonio Domínguez Ortiz, *Orto y Ocaso de Sevilla* (Seville, 1946); Pike, *Enterprise and Adventure*, c. ii.

journey; but for many others it was no more than the gateway to a new life and new opportunities on the far side of the Atlantic. It seems that some 200,000 Spaniards may have emigrated to America during the course of the sixteenth century. Some valuable work is now being done on their regional origins, but there are many other things still to be discovered about these 200,000.[1] What were their motives for going? What consequences did their emigration have for Spain? What contacts did they preserve with their homes and families, and how many of them returned?

'Three things', wrote the Frenchman Marc Lescarbot in 1609, 'induce men to seek distant lands and to leave their native homes. The first is the desire for something better. The second is when a province is so inundated with people that it overflows ... The third is divisions, quarrels and lawsuits.'[2] The publication of forty-one letters sent by Spanish settlers in the Mexican city of Puebla to their relatives in Spain provides some impression of the character and motives of the emigrants, and of the driving-force of their urge for 'something better'. A constant refrain runs through their correspondence: this is a good land. Come! 'Here you will earn more with your job in one month, than there in a year ...' writes Alonso Ramiro to his brother-in-law. Diego de San Lorente, a tailor who had arrived in Puebla in 1564, begs his wife five years later to join him with their ten-year old son. 'Here we can live according to our pleasure, and you will be very contented, and with you beside me I shall soon be rich.' Juan de Robles writes to his brother in Valladolid in 1592: 'Don't hesitate. God will help us. This land is as good as ours, for God has given us more here than there, and we shall be better off.'[3]

These were men of enterprise and initiative, willing to risk a new life in a strange environment in order to better themselves. Some may been seeking an escape from poverty. Others, like St Teresa's seven brothers, [4] may perhaps have been moved by the desire to

---

[1] Peter Boyd-Bowman, *Indice Geobiográfico de Cuarenta Mil Pobladores Españoles de América en el Siglo XVI*, i (Bogotá, 1964). For the figure of 200,000 see p. ix.
[2] *The History of New France* (3 vols., trans. and ed. Toronto, 1907–14), i, 295.
[3] Enrique Otte, 'Cartas Privadas de Puebla del Siglo XVI', *Jahrbuch für Geschichte von Staat, Wirtschaft und Gesellschaft Lateinamerikas*, iii (1966), 10–87.
[4] Valentín de Pedro, *América en las Letras Españolas del Siglo de Oro*, c. xviii.

escape from the constricting social conventions of a country where ancestry and purity of blood counted for so much. Although the numbers involved were relatively small compared with the total population of Castile, or even with the numbers of men lost to Spain by military service abroad (perhaps some eight thousand a year in the reign of Philip II),[1] the loss to Castile in terms of quality must have been considerable. If, as seems plausible, these emigrants were above the average in intelligence and ability, there could have been some loss in the genetic quality of the population as a whole. But there were important counter-balancing social and economic advantages. Many of the emigrants remitted money home. Others, the famous *Indianos* and *Peruleros*, made their fortunes in the Indies and came home again to Spain. St Teresa's brother, Lorenzo, came back as Don Lorenzo, and bought himself a property at Avila with his New World silver.[2] Some of the money from the Indies went in conspicuous consumption on a scale which amazed or scandalized even a people accustomed to opulent display. Some of it was devoted to charitable works and religious foundations, like St Teresa's convent of San José in Avila. Some of it refloated families in deep financial waters; and some of it was no doubt reinvested in agricultural or commercial enterprises.

This silver, whether it fell into the hands of Spanish aristocrats or English privateers, was Walter Prescott Webb's 'windfall' from the Great Frontier. Its presence meant a useful accretion to Europe's monetary stock, at a time when shortage of liquid capital could bring commercial or industrial ventures to an abrupt halt. Much of it was no doubt 'wasted', if economic growth is assumed to be the proper goal of every right-minded society; and its impact is better measured in terms of the changing fortunes of individuals and families, than of entire social classes. But this itself suggests something of the importance of the Indies in the life of sixteenth-century Europe. The existence of the New World gave Europeans more room for manœuvre. Above all, it promoted movement—movement of wealth, movement of people, movement of ideas. Where there was

[1] I owe this estimate to Dr N. G. Parker of Christ's College, Cambridge, who is researching on the history of the Spanish army in the Netherlands in the sixteenth and seventeenth centuries.
[2] Valentín de Pedro, pp. 267-8.

movement, there were opportunities for people with enterprise, ability, and the willingness to run risks; and they operated in a climate where success bred success. The very achievement of creating great new enterprises out of nothing, on the far side of the Atlantic, was bound to produce a new confidence in man's capacity to shape and control his world. 'We found no sugar mills when we arrived in these Indies', wrote Fernández de Oviedo, 'and all these we have built with our own hands and industry in so short a time.'[1] Similarly, Gómara expressed pride in the extent to which Hispaniola and New Spain had been 'improved' by their Spanish colonists.[2]

The opening of a new frontier on the far shores of the Atlantic therefore created new opportunities, and a climate of thought which encouraged confidence in the possibilities of success. The opportunities existed; but so also did the individuals who were ready and able to seize them. But there still remains the question of why this should have been. Was Europe's necessity in the early sixteenth century sufficient of itself to turn attention westwards, to new fields of enterprise? Or had European society already evolved certain characteristics which both enabled it to create, and make the most of, new opportunities? If either of these propositions is accepted, the frontier theory by itself cannot be regarded as an adequate explanation of the great changes in European history in the Early Modern period, and it becomes necessary to look closely at conditions in the metropolis as well as on the frontier. America may well have hastened the tempo of Europe's advance. It is even possible that the advance would not have occurred without America. But if this extreme proposition is accepted, it would still be advisable to remember the lapidary warning of Professor Braudel: 'L'Amérique ne commande pas seule.'[3] America is not in sole command.

[1] *Historia General*, i, 110.
[2] *Historia General de las Indias*, pp. 177 and 184 (the word used by Gómara is *mejorada*).
[3] Fernand Braudel, *Civilisation Matérielle et Capitalisme* (Paris, 1967), p. 352.

4

THE ATLANTIC WORLD

The Spanish conquest of America inevitably brought with it the promise of great changes in the context of European political life. The sixteenth century saw the rise of the first global empires in the history of the world. The sources of power were no longer exclusively confined to the continent of Europe itself, and the arena of conflict among European states was widened to include lands and waters far beyond Europe's traditional limits, the pillars of Hercules. Consequential changes were therefore to be expected at many different points—in the relationship between the secular authorities and a church with traditional claims to the possession of world-wide dominion; in the distribution of power both within and between states; and in ideas about power and about international relations once these were conducted in a global setting.

The problem, however, as with intellectual or economic developments in sixteenth- and early seventeenth-century Europe, is to isolate those changes directly attributable to the impact of America, from those which were already incipient or under way at the moment of discovery and conquest. It is even clearer in political than in economic life that, as Braudel said, 'L'Amérique ne commande pas seule.'[1] Indeed, it might be argued that, at least in so far as fundamental political transformations are concerned, America in the sixteenth century hardly commands at all. The refusal of states to accept the continuance of any form of subordination to a supra-national ecclesiastical authority; the absolutist tendencies of sixteenth-century princes; the development of new theories and practices to regulate the relations between independent sovereign states—all these developments are entirely conceivable in a Europe which remained in total ignorance of the existence of America. So also is some form of imperialism. The growing danger to Europe from the advance of the Ottoman Turks hinted at the desirability of a

[1] See above, p. 78.

79

concentration of power and resources in the hands of a single ruler, and the dynastic arrangements and accidents of the age conveniently brought this about. At the beginning, America was extraneous to this imperial enterprise, although in due course it came to exercise important influences upon it.

As against these underlying realities of the European political scene, the conquest and colonization of America introduced a whole new range of possibilities, which might, or might not, be brought into play. This was especially apparent in the sphere of church–state relations. At first sight, the discovery of countless millions of peoples living in spiritual darkness might have seemed to offer the church dazzling possibilities for the recovery of its prestige and authority. Throughout the sixteenth century Catholic apologists, like the German Laurentius Surius, derived consolation from the fact that, at a time when the Cross was being trampled underfoot at home, it should have been triumphantly raised in new lands overseas.[1] But the practical benefits to the church proved, in many ways, disappointing; and the process of Catholic and Counter Reformation in Europe may well have suffered from the diversion to foreign missions of some of the most enthusiastic and effective evangelists in the religious orders.

Even the Alexandrine bulls of 1493 appear in retrospect as a skilful exercise in regalism by Ferdinand the Catholic rather than a triumphant assertion of papal sovereignty. Accepting the solemn obligation imposed on the Spanish Crown to convert its new subjects in the Indies, Ferdinand and his successors contrived to extract the maximum concessions from Rome to assist them in their work. But at the same time they were careful to express no more than the most formal acknowledgement to the papacy for blessings duly received. In particular, great care came to be taken to avoid basing Spain's rights in the Indies exclusively on a papal grant. 'By donation of the Holy Apostolic See and *other just and legitimate titles*, we are lord of the West Indies, the isles and mainland of the Ocean Sea', began the law of 1519 which declared the Indies an inalienable possession of the Crown of Castile.[2] The papal bulls therefore came

---

[1] *Kurtze Chronick oder Beschreibung der vornembsten Händeln und Geschichten. . .vom Jar. . .1500 biss auf des Jar 1568. . .* (Cologne, *1568*), p. 4 v.
[2] *Recopilación de Leyes de los Reinos de las Indias* (5th ed. Madrid, 1841), lib. 3, titulo 1,

to be regarded as no more than a reinforcement of rights already won by conquest; and Spanish scholastics would follow Vitoria in arguing that since the pope was not in fact lord of the whole world, he was in no position to hand over a portion of it to the Spanish Crown.

The advancement of missionary enterprise was in any event dependent on the goodwill, and on occasions the active military assistance, of the secular power, as Acosta acknowledged when he pointed out that for missionaries to trust themselves to the mercy of peoples so barbarous as to be ignorant of the laws of nature, was like trying to make friends with wild boars or crocodiles.[1] The Spanish Crown was therefore ideally placed to dictate the ways and means of evangelization; and in so doing it could array itself in the full legal panoply conferred on it by the papacy, under the name of the *patronato*. This gave it unique authority over the disposal of ecclesiastical affairs in its American possessions—an authority for which the only European precedent was to be found in the recently conquered kingdom of Granada.[2] The marked neglect of American affairs in the discussions of the Council of Trent[3] reflects the inability of Rome to exercise any effective independent influence over the missionary work in the New World. The king of Castile, as Gómara said after listing his various ecclesiastical powers, was 'absolute lord' of the Indies.[4]

The conquest of America, then, while nominally redounding to the greater glory of God and the church of Rome, in practice enhanced the authority of the Spanish Crown, both among its own subjects and in its relations with the church. It had acquired control of immense new reserves of patronage, and it had become uniquely associated with a divine mission for the conversion of heathen peoples. But this was only one among several ways in which the acquisition of overseas territories tended to increase the power and

---

ley i. Luis Weckmann, *Las Bulas Alejandrinas de 1493 y la Teoría Política del Papado Medieval* (Mexico, 1949), pp. 246 ff., Verlinden and Pérez-Embid, *Cristóbal Colón*, pp. 85-9; Richard Konetzke, *Süd-und Mittelamerika*, 1 (Fischer Weltgeschichte vol. 22, Frankfurt, 1965), 29-35.

[1] *De Procuranda Indorum Salute*, ed. Mateos, p. 171.
[2] P. Tarsicio de Azcona, *La Elección y Reforma del Episcopado Español en Tiempo de los Reyes Católicos* (Madrid, 1960), c. vii.
[3] F. Mateos, 'Ecos de América en Trento', *Revista de Indias*, 22 (1945), 559-605.
[4] *Historia General de las Indias*, p. 291.

prestige of secular princes. The process is naturally most obvious in the Iberian peninsula, because of the priority of the Spaniards and the Portuguese in the establishment of overseas empire. But the opportunities for the extension of royal power implicit in the act of colonization are suggested by Sir Humphrey Gilbert's reply to remonstrations that he was riding roughshod over the chartered liberties of Anglo-Irish towns. 'The Prince', he said, 'had a Regular and absolute power, and that which might not be done by the one, I would do it by the other in cases of necessity.'[1] Conquest, whether in Ireland or the Indies, offered wide opportunities, and a standing temptation, to indulge in acts of absolute power. However much Spanish scholastic thought of the sixteenth century might insist on the rights of heathen states and institutions to autonomous existence, the fact remained that there was no impediment to the Spanish Crown legislating at will in matters affecting the Indies.

This freedom of action in the New World contrasted sharply with the limitations on royal power at home. It has been suggested that the decline of Castilian liberties in the Early Modern period may not be unrelated to the development of absolutist practices by the Spanish Crown in its government of the Indies.[2] This is less easily proved than suspected, but there are at least indications that their experiences in the Indies helped to encourage authoritarian tendencies among the Castilians at home in Europe. A suggestive comment is to be found scribbled on a letter sent to Philip II by the governor of Milan in 1570: 'These Italians, although they are not Indians, have to be treated as such, so that they will understand that we are in charge of them and not they in charge of us.'[3]

While the Castilian aristocracy and Castilian officials came to display the arrogance to be expected of a race of empire-builders, it was the Crown which was best placed to secure the tangible benefits of empire. It enjoyed absolute rights over the disposal of the soil and

[1] *The Voyages and Colonising Enterprises of Sir Humphrey Gilbert*, ed. D. B. Quinn (Hakluyt Society, 2nd series, vols. 83–4, London, 1940), i, 17.
[2] J. H. Parry, *The Spanish Theory of Empire in the Sixteenth Century* (Cambridge, 1940), pp. 70–5.
[3] H. G. Koenigsberger, *The Government of Sicily under Philip II of Spain* (London, 1951; emended edition, *The Practice of Empire*, Ithaca, 1969), p. 48.

subsoil of the newly conquered lands. It alone could authorize new expeditions of discovery and conquest. It possessed the right to dispose of all administrative, judicial and ecclesiastical offices in the Indies. And it had acquired vast new sources of income. In order to exploit these resources, it was compelled to devise an elaborate machinery of government which had obvious deficiencies, but which succeeded in ensuring a reasonable degree of compliance with its wishes, thousands of miles from home. According to Bacon, 'Mendoza, that was viceroy of Peru, was wont to say: That the government of Peru was the best place that the King of Spain gave, save that it was somewhat too near Madrid.'[1]

The Spanish experience in the Indies would certainly seem to confirm Walter Prescott Webb's assertion that 'frontier possessions increased both the power and prestige of the king'.[2] The prestige, the fiscal and administrative resources, and the great reserves of patronage which derived from the possession of overseas empire, all represented powerful new weapons in the armoury of the Spanish Crown as it struggled with dissident elements at home. At the same time, the dangers of domestic conflict may well have been reduced by the possession of distant territories which could provide an outlet for the energies of the unruly. This was well known to be one of the essential functions of the colonies of ancient Rome. 'By this means', wrote Bodin, 'they freed their city from beggars, mutinies, and idle persons.'[3] The lesson was not lost on those who compared the unrest and disorders of their own countries with the domestic tranquillity of Spain. 'It is an established fact', wrote the Huguenot, La Popelinière, in 1582, 'that if the Spaniard had not sent to the Indies discovered by Columbus all the rogues in his realm, and especially those who refused to return to their ordinary employment after the wars of Granada against the Moors, these would have stirred up the country or given rise to certain novelties in Spain...'[4] A great colonial enterprise could, he believed, cure France of its civil wars, just as Richard Hakluyt believed that colonization would

---

[1] *Works*, ed. Spedding, vii (London, 1859), 130–1.
[2] *The Great Frontier*, p. 147.
[3] *The Six Bookes of a Commonweale* (trans. Richard Knolles, ed. K. D. McRae, Harvard University Press, 1962), p. 656.
[4] Henri de la Popelinière, *Les Trois Mondes* (Paris, 1582), avant-discours.

improve the health of the English body politic by siphoning off a surplus population that was all too prone to sedition.[1]

These contemporary assumptions seem plausible enough. There was presumably less inducement to fight for opportunities and rights at home if these could be secured at less cost by emigration overseas. Just as the authoritarian tendencies of the sixteenth- and seventeenth-century state may have encouraged the disaffected to emigrate, so, in turn, their emigration may have enhanced the prospects of authoritarianism at home. Obedience to authority, and a high degree of social conformity, were perhaps the price to be paid in the mother country for empire overseas.

It was ironical that it should have been a natural rebel, Hernán Cortés, who showed himself the first man to have a clear vision of the possibilities of colonial empire as a means of enhancing the prestige and power of his prince. It was typical of the genius of Cortés, not only that he should have grasped that colonization was the key to empire, but also that he should have set the downfall of Montezuma into a global context by relating it to that other great event of the climactic year 1519—the election of Charles of Ghent to the Imperial throne. Within a few months, Charles had succeeded not to one empire but to two; and according to Cortés he could call himself Emperor of New Spain, the former realm of Montezuma, 'with no less reason and title than he did of Germany, which by the grace of God Your Majesty possesses'. Indeed, for this very purpose, Cortés had carefully arranged an 'imperial donation' by Montezuma, although he conveniently lost the papers recording this singular act of state. This unprecedented accretion of titles and power, both in Mexico and Germany, was a clear indication to Cortés of the providential mission for which his royal master was inexorably destined. He was now on his way to becoming 'monarch of the world', and the king of France and all the other princes would be compelled to subject themselves to his imperial power.[2]

[1] 'Discourse of Western Planting' (1584), in E. G. R. Taylor, *The Original Writings and Correspondence of the Two Richard Hakluyts* (Hakluyt Society, 2nd series, vol. 77, London, 1935), vol. ii, document 46. See also G. V. Scammell, 'The New Worlds and Europe in the Sixteenth Century', *TheHistorical Journal*, xii (1969), 407.

[2] Hernán Cortés, *Cartas y Documentos*, pp. 33, 229, 236; R. Konetzke, 'Hernán Cortés como poblador de la Nueva España', *Estudios Cortesianos* (Madrid, 1948), pp. 341–81;

Cortés's vision of universal monarchy was shared by eminent figures in the Imperial entourage. But none of them seems to have glimpsed, as he did, the way in which Charles's overseas possessions could give a new dimension to the old imperial theme. The inspiration of Charles V's imperialism, like his Empire itself, remained obstinately European. Charles displayed no interest in assuming a new title of Emperor of the Indies or New Spain. Nor did the Imperial ideal commend itself to the Spanish scholastics. Vitoria devoted a section of his *De Indis* to refuting the thesis that the Emperor could be lord of the whole world, and Sepúlveda never used the Imperial argument to justify Spanish rule over Indians.[1]

The absence of enthusiasm for Cortés's global vision of empire may suggest a certain parochialism on the part of Charles and the Spaniards of his generation. But it reflects also the realities of power in the world of Charles V. His empire remained a European empire because the sources of its strength were overwhelmingly European. Between 1521 and 1544 the mines in the Habsburg hereditary lands produced almost four times as much silver as the whole of America.[2] It was only in Charles's later years, between 1545 and the late 1550s, that these figures were reversed. Even then, there were wild fluctuations in the remittances to Seville, with really substantial quantities arriving only after 1550, as the troubles in Peru drew to a close. It is necessary, too, to maintain a sense of proportion about the over-all contribution made by America to Charles's revenues as silver production increased. In 1554, for instance, the Crown's American revenue represented only 11 per cent of its total income.[3] Over the years the American remittances for the Crown averaged out at some 250,000 ducats a year—a figure which would scarcely have been sufficient to compensate for the fall in the Crown's traditional sources of revenue within Spain, brought about by the decline in the value of money.

V. Frankl, 'Imperio particular e imperio universal en las cartas de relación de Hernán Cortés', *Cuadernos Hispanoamericanos* (1963); J. H. Elliott, 'The Mental World of Hernán Cortés', *Transactions of the Royal Historical Society*, 5th series, 17 (1967), 41–58.

[1] *De Indis*, I, 2, 2; Joseph Höffner, *Christentum und Menschenwürde. Das Anliegen der Spanischen Kolonialethik im Goldenen Zeitalter* (Trier, 1947), p. 219.
[2] Juan Friede, *Los Welser* (Caracas–Madrid, 1961), p. 577, note 6 to chapter v.
[3] John Lynch, *Spain under the Habsburgs*, i (Oxford, 1964), 129

But this kind of assessment is likely to give a misleading impression of America's real significance for the empire of Charles V. Charles's imperialism was made possible by deficit financing, and it was the attraction of the American connection, and the bait of American silver, which provided an important inducement to the great financial houses to advance money to the Emperor on such a massive scale over so many years. The New World, then, helped to *sustain* Europe's first great imperial adventure of the sixteenth century, even if it did not originally launch it. It is impossible to guess how long the adventure could have continued without the silver of the Indies; but we know that, in the 1540s and early 1550s, there was a decisive shift in the centre of economic gravity of Charles's empire, away from the Netherlands and Germany to the Iberian peninsula. From 1553 the Genoese had gained the lead over German and Flemish bankers in advancing loans to the Emperor.[1] The change was symbolic of the eclipse of the old financial world of Antwerp and Augsburg, and its replacement by a new financial nexus linking Genoa to Seville and the silver mines of America. Charles's increasing dependence on the resources of Spain and the Indies during those last traumatic years of his reign indicates that it was about this time that the New World became decisive for the continuation of his Empire in the Old.

But in the end the New World, like everything else, failed him. M. Chaunu has taught us to set the Imperial abdication, the royal bankruptcies of the late 1550s, and the peace of Cateau-Cambrésis into the global context of a drastic slump in the transatlantic trade.[2] Here again, though, it is not clear whether we should turn first to America or to Europe for an explanation of the crisis. No doubt this was a time of transition for the New World, as the age of easy plunder came to an end. But it was also a time in which the activities of French privateers played havoc with Seville's transatlantic trade, and in which Charles's financial demands increased as extravagantly

---

[1] Ramón Carande, *Carlos V y sus Banqueros*, iii (Madrid, 1967), 405. The idea of a shift in the centre of economic gravity in the middle years of the sixteenth century is suggested by F. Braudel, *La Méditerranée*, pp. 518–25, and has since been developed by Braudel himself and by other historians. See also Pierre Chaunu, 'Séville et la "Belgique", 1555–1648', *Revue du Nord*, xlii (1960), 259–92, especially 269–71.
[2] *Séville et l'Atlantique*, viii (ii,i), 255–352.

as his debts. In 1556 he confiscated all the bullion arriving at Seville for private individuals. The disastrous state of his finances was driving him to strangle the goose which laid the silver eggs.

With the return of peace in Europe, and the recovery and expansion of the transatlantic trade after 1562, Habsburg imperialism reconstituted itself in a new form, more appropriate to the times. Philip II's empire revolved around the axis of Seville, in the sense that the royal credit fluctuated with the remittances of American silver, and to some extent also with the more general movements of Seville's transatlantic trade. In the second half of the sixteenth century it is legitimate—as it is not really legitimate for the first half of the century—to speak of an Atlantic economy and an Atlantic empire. In this respect, Philip II's empire, and that of his successors, differs fundamentally from that of Charles V. Charles's empire was always firmly continental. The empire of the Philips was, almost in spite of themselves, maritime and global.

Yet the implications of this only gradually became apparent to contemporaries, and seem never to have been fully grasped by Philip II himself. It was Castile and Italy, in any event, which still provided the bulk of his revenues, although with annual remittances for the Crown running at over two million ducats by the 1590s, the Indies accounted for between a fifth and a quarter of the Crown's income during the final years of the reign. But it was not easy, especially from the heart of Castile, to adjust to a world in which sea-power was the key to the preservation of empire, and in which silver was most likely to benefit those who knew how to make it work.

Nothing could alter the fact, however, that the whole context of international political life had begun to change. 'We see what floods of treasure have flowed into Europe by that action', wrote Bacon, surveying the results of the conquest of the Indies. 'Besides, infinite is the access of territory and empire by the same enterprise.'[1] This was bound to affect the balance of power both within Europe itself, and between Europe and its traditional enemy, Islam. It is possible that the Spanish commitment to the conquest of the Indies during the first half of the sixteenth century prevented the mounting of a

[1] 'Advertisement touching an Holy Warre' (1622), *Works*, vii, 20.

sustained onslaught against the Turks and their allies in North Africa and the Mediterranean. But, by the second half of the century, the investment in overseas empire was beginning to yield its profits, even in the war against Islam. The Ottoman Empire now found itself confronted by a Spanish empire fresh from its triumphs over distant peoples, and with great new reserves of silver at its command. In the circumstances, it was scarcely surprising that a society which had traditionally displayed very little curiosity about the non-Islamic world should have begun at this point to show some signs of interest in the historical reasons for the expansion of Spanish power.[1] Around 1580 a *History of the West Indies* was written for the Sultan Murad III. Its author seems to have relied upon Italian translations of the works of Peter Martyr, Fernández de Oviedo and Gómara, together with Zárate's *History of the Conquest of Peru*. 'Within twenty years', he wrote, 'the Spanish people conquered all the islands and captured forty thousand people, and killed thousands of them. Let us hope to God that some time these valuable lands will be conquered by the family of Islam, and will be inhabited by Moslems and become part of the Ottoman lands.'[2] The hope seemed to bear little relation to reality as the balance of power in the decades after Lepanto began to tilt decisively against Islam.

Whether for the Ottoman Empire or for the states of Christendom, the power of Spain appeared to be the overwhelming fact of European international life in the eighty years between 1560 and 1640. It is clear now, as it was clear to contemporaries, that this power was intimately related to Spain's possession of rich overseas territories. But the exact way in which this relationship affected the formulation and execution of Spanish foreign policy is still something of a mystery. The most ambitious attempt to explain the rise and fall of Spanish power in terms of America is that of M. Chaunu, who has attempted to illustrate in detail how the highpoints of Philip II's imperialism coincided with the period of maximum growth in

---

[1] *Historians of the Middle East*, ed. B. Lewis and P. M. Holt (London, 1962), p. 184.
[2] I am indebted to Dr Thomas D. Goodrich for information about the sources used for the *Tarih-i Hind-i garbi*, which he examines in his unpublished Ph.D. dissertation for Columbia University, *Sixteenth-Century Ottoman Americana*. I am also very grateful to Mr Saleh Özbaran for discussions about this work, and for translating this passage for me.

Seville's trade with the Indies, and how in turn the gradual retreat from war under Philip III coincided with increasing difficulties in the Spanish Atlantic system. But the correlation of movements of the Indies trade with changes in Spanish foreign policy is an exercise beset with pitfalls, as M. Chaunu himself would be the first to admit. To use his own words, 'the correlations are clear, but their exact meaning is difficult to disentangle'.[1] Does trade cease to expand, for instance, because of the disruptions caused by war, or does war come to an end because the trade which nurtures it is running into difficulties? The answer would seem to be both.

For all the subtlety of M. Chaunu's arguments, there does seem to be some danger of an excessively mechanical interpretation of political actions as a kind of Pavlovian response to commercial fluctuations, some of them very short-term in character. An instructive example is provided by his interesting attempt to link the last great manifestation of Spanish imperialism—intervention in Germany at the start of the Thirty Years War—with a brief revival of prosperity at Seville between 1616 and 1619.[2] This would be more convincing if there were any sign of awareness among Philip III's advisers that financial conditions at this moment were unusually favourable, and that the chances of obtaining credit were good. But no such awareness is apparent in the papers of the Council of Finance, which was presumably in some position to gauge the general financial climate. On the contrary, its memoranda for these years were more than usually gloomy, even for that professionally gloomy body. In document after document the President of the Council warned the duke of Lerma that the financial situation was quite exceptionally grave. The Crown's silver revenues from the Indies had unexpectedly slumped to below a million ducats a year, and the President insisted that Spain was in no condition to embark on heavy new expenditures in Germany. But the royal reply was conclusive: 'These provisions are so vital that the Council of Finance must find them. Germany cannot possibly be abandoned.'[3] There may have been many good reasons for Spanish intervention in

[1] *Séville et l'Atlantique*, viii (ii, ii), 888.   [2] 'Séville et la "Belgique"', p. 291.
[3] J. H. Elliott, *The Revolt of the Catalans* (Cambridge, 1963), pp. 189–90.

Germany, but the decision was certainly not based on any rational assessment of financial possibilities, related to a consideration of favourable economic trends.

It could, of course, be argued that the final determinant of policy lay less with the decisions of ministers, whether rationally or irrationally reached, than with the willingness and capacity of bankers to advance more money to the Spanish Crown. But this was dependent on many variables, of which the prosperity of Seville's trade with the Indies was not necessarily, or always, the most important. One of the reasons, for instance, for Philip II's ability to raise such large loans in the 1590s, seems to have been that wartime conditions restricted the field for investment, and left merchants with liquid capital which they were prepared to lend to the Crown at the high rates of interest prevailing.[1] Spanish power, then, was made up of a whole complex of considerations and circumstances, which bore different relations to each other at different times. Alongside the tangibles—strong armies, numerous territorial possessions and a wide variety of revenues—there were also the intangibles of credit and confidence.

Yet the fact remains that it was the silver of the Indies which gave cohesion and movement to the mighty machine. This inescapable fact impressed, and indeed over-impressed, contemporaries. 'With this great treasure did not the Emperor Charles get from the French king the kingdom of Naples, the dukedom of Milan and all his other dominions in Italy, Lombardy, Piedmont and Savoy? With this treasure did he not take the pope prisoner? and sacked the see of Rome?' These questions, quoted in Hakluyt's 'Discourse of Western Planting' from a memorandum addressed to the counts of Emden,[2] illustrate the obsessive preoccupation of the age with the silver of the Indies as the key to Spanish power. From the days of Hakluyt to those of Oliver Cromwell, the well-worn theme was reproduced time and time again. 'They are not his great territories which make him so powerfull', said Sir Benjamin Rudyard in the House of Commons in 1624. '... For it is very well knowne, that Spaine itself is but weake in men, and barren of naturall commodities ... No sir, they are his mines in the West Indies, which

---

[1] Henri Lapeyre, *Simon Ruiz et les Asientos de Philippe II* (Paris, 1953), p. 104.
[2] *Original Writings*, ed. Taylor, ii, 243.

minister fuell to feed his vast ambitious desire of universall monarchy.'[1]

The Indies, then, could be brought easily enough within the radius of the received doctrine of the sixteenth-century state, that money was the sinews of war. But certain conclusions were drawn from this which gradually enlarged the boundaries of conventional wisdom about the character and the seat of national power. If the source of Spain's strength was located in its transatlantic possessions, the Spanish Monarchy might be more easily overthrown by action overseas than at home. Intercept the silver on its way to Seville, and the king of Spain would no longer have the capacity to maintain his armies in the field.

Although French privateers had been active in the Atlantic during the first half of the century,[2] the idea was only gradually transformed into a broad strategic design. It seems to have been during the 1550s that various lines of interest began to converge onto the central theme of the Indies and their relationship to Spanish power. The resumption of the conflict between Charles V and the French in 1552 was followed by some daring and successful raids by French corsairs in the Caribbean. Three years later, French colonial projects, which had begun abortively in Canada in the 1540s, were revived in Villegaignon's expedition to Brazil, under the patronage of Admiral Coligny.[3]

At the same time as interest in the New World was quickening in France, it was also quickening in an England which had entered the Spanish orbit with the marriage of Mary Tudor to Philip. English merchants engaged in the Spanish trade were building up a stock of information about America. New facts became available to a wider public through the translations of Richard Eden, which included the first three of Peter Martyr's *Decades* in 1555.[4] These in turn attracted the attention and stimulated the imagination of men who were

[1] L. F. Stock, *Proceedings and Debates of the British Parliaments respecting North America*, i (Washington, 1924), 62.
[2] A. P. Newton, *The European Nations in the West Indies, 1493–1688* (London, 1933, reprinted 1966), pp. 49 ff.
[3] For French colonizing projects in the sixteenth century see especially C. A. Julien, *Les Débuts de l'Expansion et de la Colonisation Française* (Paris, 1947).
[4] G. B. Parks, *Richard Hakluyt and the English Voyages* (New York, 1928), cs. i and ii.

becoming obsessed with the religious and political consequences of the growth of Spanish power. Sir Peter Carew, who fled to Rouen after the collapse of the Western Rising in 1554, brooded in his exile on the riches that Spain derived from the Indies. His copy of Eden's translation of the *Decades* bore heavy annotations in the chapters dealing with navigation between Spain and America. It was perhaps from this same copy, too, that a fellow-exile, John Ponet, obtained the information about the destruction of the American Indians with which he illustrated the consequences of tyranny in his *Short Treatise of Politicke Power*.[1]

On both sides of the Channel, then, at much the same time, similar preoccupations were beginning to build a consensus of ideas, which would influence the course of international relations for the next hundred years or more. These ideas were developed in a continuing dialogue between Englishmen and Frenchmen, many of them united by ties of friendship and religion, and still more of them united by their detestation of Spain. In 1558, Henry II was considering a project, probably inspired by Coligny, for a surprise attack on the Isthmus of Panama and the capture of the silver supplies from Peru and New Spain.[2] After the treaty of Cateau-Cambrésis, Coligny's interest shifted to schemes for the colonization of Florida; and Ribault's visit to England in 1563 to secure English support for the project did much to arouse English interest in the possibilities of settlement in North America.[3]

It was out of the events of these years and the reactions to them—the shock of the Florida massacre and of the discomfiture of Hawkins at San Juan de Ulúa—that there emerged the various elements of the Protestant grand design. After Coligny's murder, his plans for striking at Spain through the Indies were kept alive by Duplessis-Mornay and William of Orange. Duplessis-Mornay's proposal of 1584 for the reduction of Spanish power vividly illustrates how statesmen were beginning, like the sea-captains before them, to

[1] Winthrop S. Hudson, *John Ponet* (Chicago, 1942), p. 84; Christina Garrett, *The Marian Exiles* (Cambridge, 1938, reprinted 1966), pp. 105 ff. For Ponet on the Spaniards in the Indies, see pp. (93)–(94), sig, F. vii and F. vii v, of the *Short Treatise*, reproduced in facsimile in Hudson's *John Ponet*.
[2] Newton, *European Nations in the West Indies*, pp. 58–9.
[3] Quinn, *Voyages of Gilbert*, i, 4–5; Rowse, *The Elizabethans and America*, p. 13.

grasp the importance of sea-power and to think in global terms. If the French seized Majorca, he argued, they could intercept Spanish silver on its way to Italy. And if they attacked the isthmus of Panama, they could intercept it at source. At the same time, they would be posed for a descent on the Pacific, which could make them masters of the spice trade of the East.[1]

For all the efforts of Hawkins, Oxenham and Drake, such ambitious designs proved to be impossibly grandiose. Spanish power in the New World was too formidable, and the silver convoys too well protected, for Protestant hopes of taking Spain 'by way of the Indies'[2] to be realized in the reign of Philip II. Nor was there any immediate future in establishing colonies as bases from which to raid the Spanish Indies: if colonies were to be established, they were best established for other and stronger reasons, and well away from areas under Spanish physical control. But by the 1580s English raids were beginning to strike a pattern.[3] The onslaughts in the Atlantic may not have been sufficiently co-ordinated to acquire the status of a systematic offensive, but they were at least based on a common assumption that Spain's colonial empire was the source of its economic strength. It was this assumption, too, which helped to dictate Philip II's response, for the objective of the Spanish Armada was, in the words of the king's secretary, 'no less the security of the Indies than the recovery of the Netherlands'.[4]

It was only slowly, and with considerable uncertainty, that colonial and oceanic ambitions began to impose themselves on the more traditional causes of rivalry of West European states. In the later sixteenth and early seventeenth centuries, the New World still remained on the fringe of European conflicts. Yet the very fact that these conflicts were being extended into the waters of the Atlantic and the Caribbean, and even the Pacific, meant that new opportunities for international friction were constantly being created.

1 *Mémoires et Correspondance de Duplessis-Mornay*, ii, (Paris, 1824), doc. xcvii.
2 The words used by the French Huguenot leader La Noue in a letter of 17 August 1588 to Sir Francis Walsingham, printed in Henri Hauser, *François de la Noue* (Paris, 1892), pp. 315–19.
3 G. S. Graham, *The Politics of Naval Supremacy* (Cambridge, 1965), pp. 10–12. But for the continuing lack of system, see K. R. Andrews, *Drake's Voyages* (London, 1967), p. 96.
4 Juan de Idiáquez, quoted by John Lynch, *Spain under the Habsburgs*, i, 315.

The process was aggravated by the fact that the New World was finding a place in national mythologies. To the Castilians, the discovery and possession of the Indies was further, and conclusive, evidence that they were the chosen race. It was not surprising that a nation which saw itself entrusted with a great civilizing mission among the barbarous peoples of America should presume to set standards to be followed by the rest of mankind. This idea was encouraged by an ancient and well-established tradition about the march of human history. Through the early church fathers and Otto of Freising, sixteenth-century Europe had inherited the classical notion that world-power and civilization moved gradually from east to west.[1] To a Spanish humanist, like Pérez de Oliva, the conclusion was obvious. The empires of the Persians and the Chaldeans had been replaced in turn by those of Egypt, Greece, Italy and France, and now by that of Spain. Here the centre of the world would remain, 'checked by the sea, and so well guarded that it cannot escape'.[2] But others were not so sure. In his narrative of 1583 describing Sir Humphrey Gilbert's last voyage, Edward Hayes argued that 'the countreys lying north of Florida, God hath reserved the same to be reduced unto Christian civility by the English nation'. This, he thought, was made 'very probable by the revolution and cause of God's word and religion, which from the beginning hath moved from the East, towards, and at last unto the West, where it is like to end'.[3] By the closing decades of the sixteenth century it was clear that the Spaniards were not the only people in the world to cherish the vision of a mission, and an empire, in the west.

By encouraging an appetite for treasure, trade and colonies, and then conferring upon it the sanction of a providential mission, America played its part in fostering the nationalism of sixteenth-century states. At the same time, incidents in the New World themselves provided new images on which national and religious hatreds could thrive. The atrocities of Drake entered the collective mentality of the Castilians, just as the Florida massacre or the San Juan de

---

[1] John M. Headley, *Luther's View of Church History* (New Haven, 1963), pp. 240–1; Glacken, *Traces on the Rhodian Shore*, pp. 276–8.
[2] Pérez de Oliva, *Obras*, f. 134.
[3] Quinn, *Voyages of Gilbert*, ii, 387–8. See also Sanford, *The Quest for Paradise*, p. 51.

Ulúa affair entered the collective mentality of the England of Eliza beth. But, in the nature of things, the Spaniards offered many more hostages to fortune than their rivals. Although the Black Legend possessed a long, if hardly respectable, European ancestry, the Spanish record in the Indies gave it a new and terrifying lustre. Even in the earliest histories of the conquest, like Peter Martyr's *Decades*, there was material enough for the indictment of the conquerors; but two works published in the middle decades of the century documented the Spanish record in a conveniently summary form. Las Casas's *Brief Account of the Destruction of the Indies*, first published in Spain in 1552, and Girolamo Benzoni's racy *History of the New World* (Venice, 1565) provided between them as much ammunition as even the most fanatical enemies of Spain could have wished. Both these books began to secure a European public at the time when the conflict between Spain and the northern powers, and between Rome and Geneva, was approaching its climax. A Latin edition of Benzoni, published in Geneva in 1578, was followed by German and French translations in 1579. In 1579, too, an account of the Florida massacre was also published in Geneva, and Las Casas appeared in Dutch and French translations, before being translated into English in 1583. By the early 1580s, therefore, the most lurid information about Spanish conduct in the Indies was circulating through the continent. It needed only the horrific illustrations of Theodore de Bry's new editions of Las Casas at the end of the century to stamp an indelible image of Spanish atrocities on the European consciousness.[1]

The Huguenots, the Dutch and the English all seized on Benzoni and Las Casas with glee. In William of Orange's *Apology* of 1581, the destruction of twenty million Indians was duly brought forward as evidence of the innate propensity of the Spaniards to commit acts of unspeakable cruelty.[2] Against propaganda warfare on this scale,

[1] Sverker Arnoldsson, *La Leyenda Negra* (Göteborg, 1960), for the European origins of the Black Legend. For its American extension, see especially Rómulo D. Carbia, *Historia de la Leyenda Negra Hispanoamericana* (Madrid, 1944), and the suggestive article by Pierre Chaunu, 'La Légende Noire Antihispanique', *Revue de Psychologie des Peuples* (Université de Caen, 1964), pp. 188–223. I am grateful to Dr A. W. Lovett for bringing this article to my notice.
[2] French version (Leyden, 1581), p. 50.

Spain's official chronicler of the Indies could offer no more than feeble resistance. A weapon had been forged in those years of European crisis which would render invaluable service to generations of enemies of Spain. The sufferings of the Indians even figured in the pamphlet campaign of the Catalans against the tyrannical government of Olivares in the revolt of 1640,[1] and it was in Barcelona that Las Casas received the accolade of his first Spanish reprint, in 1646.[2]

For the first time in European history, the colonial record of an imperial power was being systematically used against it by its enemies. But the crude propaganda of foreign enemies was perhaps in the long run less debilitating to Spanish morale than the increasing doubts of Spaniards themselves about the value to them of the Indies. Sixteenth-century complaints about high prices and the pernicious moral consequences of sudden riches gave way to an increasing number of informed and perceptive comments about the nature and the use of wealth. There was widespread appreciation that Spain itself saw very little of the American silver, and that, in the words of that bitterly anti-American Spaniard, Suárez de Figueroa, 'our Spain is the Indies of the Genoese'.[3] But there was also a strong current of anti-bullionist sentiment,[4] brilliantly represented in the work of the great *arbitrista*, González de Cellorigo. 'Our Spain', he argued, 'has concentrated on the trade of the Indies, from which come gold and silver, and has neglected trade with neighbouring kingdoms. If all the gold and silver that has been and is being found there were to flow into it, it would still not be so rich or so powerful as it would be without them.'[5] For González, true wealth lay in trade and agriculture and industry, and in riches productively used. There were many who agreed with him. In the same year, 1600, Luis Valle de la Cerda, who advocated a system of public banks, insisted that without such banks to foster economic

1 *Secrets Públichs* (Barcelona, 1641), article 2 (no page numbers).
2 Ramón Menéndez Pidal, *El Padre Las Casas* (Madrid, 1963), p. 364.
3 Cristóbal Suárez de Figueroa, *El Passagero* (1617, ed. Madrid, 1914), p. 20.
4 See Pierre Vilar, *Crecimiento y Desarollo*, pp. 175–207 for a penetrating study of Spanish attitudes to bullion.
5 *Memorial de la política necessaria y útil restauración a la república de España* (Valladolid, 1600), p. 15 v.

development the Indies were 'nothing but the ruin of our greatness and of the ancient majesty of Spain'. Thanks to the Indies, the oceans teemed with ships bearing gold and silver, which merely brought fresh power and sustenance to Spain's enemies.[1]

Castile's misfortunes were compounded by the fact that disillusionment with the supposed benefits of overseas empire came at a time when the burdens of empire were becoming increasingly heavy to bear. If the reasons for Spain's decline lie deeply embedded in Spain itself, and not least in its traditional attitude to the employment of wealth, the phenomenon of decline still needs to be set into the wider context of the Atlantic world as a whole.[2] Between 1621 and 1641 the Spanish Atlantic empire was beginning to collapse.[3] This collapse is partly explicable in terms of the decline of silver remittances from the Indies, and the dwindling of Seville's Atlantic trade. But these in turn must be related to the fresh involvement of Spain in international conflict, after the relatively peaceful reign of Philip III, and to the failure of Spain to learn adequately the lesson of the later sixteenth century that 'he who possesses the sea will have dominion over the land'.[4]

It was a measure of the changes which had occurred since the days of Philip II that the New World was increasingly drawn into the European struggle of the 1620s and 1630s, and that there was a close and constant interplay between events in America and Europe during the final years of Spanish power. It was in these years that the traditional power-struggle of Europe at last acquired a genuine transatlantic extension. The pattern of the Atlantic conflict was determined by the complex triangular relationship between Castile, Portugal and the Dutch. Spain's decision to resume the war with the United Provinces in 1621 was determined at least as much by concern for its overseas interests as by the hopeless determination to crush a rebellion which had already lasted for half a century. It was argued that the renewal of war in Europe would reduce Dutch

---

[1] *Desempeño del Patrimonio de Su Magestad* (Madrid, 1600), p. 157 v.
[2] These words were written before the appearance of vol. ii of John Lynch, *Spain under the Habsburgs*, which shows a clear appreciation of this wider context.
[3] The collapse is documented in Chaunu, *Séville et l'Atlantique*, vol. viii (ii, ii), cinquième partie, on which I have drawn for the paragraphs that follow.
[4] Suárez de Figueroa, *El Passagero*, p. 48.

opportunities for those overseas activities which had done such damage to the Spanish and Portuguese colonial empires during the twelve-years truce.[1]

The fallacy of this argument was cruelly exposed in 1624, when the Dutch attack, which had previously been concentrated on West Africa and Portugal's Far Eastern empire, switched to Brazil. The ejection of the Dutch from Bahia at once became for Olivares a matter of the highest urgency. There were sound political as well as economic reasons for his deep concern. The development of Portugal's Atlantic empire, based on the rapid expansion of the Brazilian sugar industry, was helping to compensate for the loss of its Far Eastern trade to the Dutch. The Portuguese had been defeated in the East Indies, in spite of the presumed strength of the Spanish Monarchy, to which they found themselves reluctantly joined. If they were now to be defeated in Brazil, too, the uneasy union of the Crowns of Castile and Portugal would be still further undermined. In sending a powerful combined Spanish and Portuguese expeditionary force to recapture Bahia in 1625, Olivares therefore had his eye at least as much on the internal political arrangements of the Spanish Monarchy as on Brazilian sugar and African slaves.[2]

Thwarted in Brazil, the Dutch were forced back into the waters of the Caribbean, where the most spectacular of their achievements was Piet Heyn's capture of the treasure fleet in 1628. The dream of Coligny, William of Orange and Duplessis-Mornay had been realized at last, and at a moment of the most acute embarrassment for Spain. The loss of expected revenues from the treasure fleet, at a time when he was becoming embroiled in the War of the Mantuan Succession, forced Olivares to sequester a million ducats in silver reaching Seville for private individuals in 1629.[3] The sequestration in turn

---

[1] The argument used, among others, by Don Carlos Coloma (A. Rodríguez Villa, *Ambrosio Spínola*, Madrid, 1904, p. 387).

[2] For the relationship of Spain, Portugal and the United Provinces in these years, see C. R. Boxer, 'Spaniards and Portuguese in the Iberian colonial world', *Liber Amicorum Salvador de Madariaga* (Bruges, 1966), pp. 239-51, and, by the same author, *Salvador de Sá and the Struggle for Brazil and Angola, 1602-1686* (London, 1952); *The Dutch in Brazil, 1624-1654* (London 1957); and *The Portuguese Seaborne Empire, 1415-1826* (London, 1969), c. v. For the Portuguese Atlantic in general, F. Mauro, *Le Portugal et l'Atlantique au XVIIe siècle, 1570-1670* (Paris, 1960).

[3] Antonio Domínguez Ortiz, *Política y Hacienda de Felipe IV* (Madrid, 1960), pp. 287-9; Lynch, *Spain under the Habsburgs*, ii, 74.

undermined the confidence of Seville's merchant community, and reduced its inclination and ability to reinvest in the Indies trade.

The silver which might have financed a successful Spanish campaign in Italy helped instead to finance a new Dutch attack on Brazil in 1630.[1] This time Olivares lacked the resources to mobilize an expeditionary force powerful enough to eject them from Pernambuco before they became entrenched. Dutch occupation of northeastern Brazil in the early 1630s had serious consequences for the conduct of Spanish foreign policy in Europe, where Olivares was becoming increasingly anxious to reach a settlement with the United Provinces because of the imminent prospect of war with France. His freedom of diplomatic manœuvre was drastically restricted by the problem of Brazil, which he could not afford to abandon to the Dutch because of the inevitable reaction in Portugal.[2]

This reaction was likely to be all the more violent because of the growing friction in relations between Castile and Portugal during the 1630s. The successful infiltration of Portuguese merchants into the economic life of the Spanish Indies, followed by their entry onto the scene as bankers for the Spanish Crown from 1626–7, produced an upsurge of anti-Portuguese sentiment in Spain and America. They were worse than the Genoese, wrote Pellicer, as he catalogued their crimes.[3] The bonds of mutual interest which had done something to cement the union of the Crowns in the decades after 1580 were therefore already being loosened before the formal break in December 1640. The defence of Portugal's Brazilian empire was proving an increasing financial, military and diplomatic embarrassment to Castile, and at the same time it felt growing resentment at Portuguese exploitation of its American wealth. The Portuguese, for their part, discovered that they were increasingly unwanted in Spanish America at the same time as they were threatened with the loss of their own possessions in Brazil. Many of them may justifiably have felt that they could hardly do worse on their own than they were doing with the benefit of help from Castile. Some, no doubt,

---

[1] Newton, *The European Nations*, p. 153.
[2] See Fritz Dickmann, *Der Westfälische Frieden* (Münster, 1959), p. 261.
[3] *Comercio Impedido*, p. 5.

glimpsed the possibilities of an independent Portuguese Atlantic empire, based on Africa and Brazil, as a substitute for a declining Spanish Atlantic empire, based on the Indies and Seville.

It was in 1639–40 that the interaction of events in the Old World and the New reached a climax which effectively destroyed the Spanish Monarchy as a great international power. The strain imposed on Castile's resources by the war with France compelled Olivares to intervene repeatedly in the commercial life of Seville; and by 1639 his fiscal activities had virtually paralysed the trade with the Indies. Naval defeat at the Battle of the Downs in October 1639 was followed by naval defeat in Brazilian waters in January 1640. Spain had patently lost command of the seas, and during 1640 no treasure fleet reached Seville. In the spring of 1640 the Catalans revolted; in August the Spanish armies, starved of money, suffered new defeats in Flanders; in December, Portugal proclaimed its independence. In turn, the disintegration of Spanish power, both in northern Europe and the Iberian peninsula itself, left the Caribbean wide open to incursions by the English, the French and the Dutch.

It was in the 1640s, then, after a century and a half of tenacious resistance, that the exclusive Iberian monopoly of the New World effectively came to an end. But what right did the Iberian powers ever have to such a monopoly? If their claim rested on papal donation, the French and the English could justifiably ask who gave popes the right to divide up the world in this way. Francis I's remark to the Imperial ambassador in 1540 that he would like to see Adam's last will and testament was in fact something more than an impudent debating-point.[1] The discovery and conquest of America had raised new and difficult problems for the European international community, and particularly that of just titles to newly-discovered lands. Francis I insisted, by no means unreasonably, that the sun shone as much for him as for anyone else, and argued that the seas were open and that possession of land should rest on effective occupation. But as far as Spain was concerned, this argument was not open to discussion. The New World was ignored in the peace settlements of Cateau-Cambrésis and Vervins, although by a verbal

[1] Julien, *Les Débuts de l'Expansion*, pp. 145–7; Roland Mousnier, *Les XVIe et XVIIe Siècles* (Paris, 1954), p. 136.

agreement of 1559 the peace of Cateau-Cambrésis did not extend to non-European waters (or, as later generations expressed it, 'beyond the Line').[1]

Even a century after the discovery, therefore, no real progress had been made in incorporating the New World into a fixed framework of international relations. But this was becoming increasingly necessary as it grew clear that there were vast tracts of America which Spain was incapable either of colonizing or defending. It was this inability of Spain in the seventeenth century to sustain its claim to exclusive dominion which gradually forced on it the *de facto* acceptance of effective occupation as sufficient title to overseas possession. This acceptance, implicit in the treaty of Münster of 1648, and more explicitly stated in the Anglo-Spanish treaty of Madrid of 1670,[2] was the inevitable outcome of Spain's military defeat.

But it was one of the ironies of the situation that the theoretical justification for Spanish monopoly based on papal donation had long since been undermined by the Spaniards themselves. The rejection of the doctrine of direct papal power by Vitoria, Suárez and other leading Spanish scholastics of the sixteenth century, had left a central weakness in the Spanish defences which their alternative arguments could not fully repair.[3] It was not clear, for instance, why Vitoria should proclaim man's natural right to trade with, and settle in, all parts of the world, and then should proceed to deny this right to other nations once it had been exercised by Spaniards in the Indies. In the circumstances, it is hardly surprising that the Spaniards, like their opponents, should increasingly have argued, in so far as they bothered to argue at all, from the premise of prior discovery and conquest.

But the very scholars who had challenged the thesis of the papal donation had also begun to elaborate an alternative framework into which the problem of international rights could eventually be set. Vitoria had insisted on the autonomy of all the peoples of the world,

[1] Garrett Mattingly, 'No peace beyond what line?', *Transactions of the Royal Historical Society*, 5th series, 13 (1963), 145–62.
[2] Newton, *The European Nations*, pp. 202 and 269–70.
[3] J. H. Parry, *The Age of Reconnaissance* (London, 1963), pp. 318–19.

even if they were heathen, and had proclaimed the existence of an international community, a republic of the world. Suárez showed that this community was a community of states whose relations should be regulated by the *jus gentium*.[1] Alfonso de Castro argued, around 1550, that by the law of nations the sea could not be the exclusive preserve of any single state.[2] These ideas, reformulated and amplified by Grotius, provided a legal and theoretical structure for the conduct of international relations—a structure which afforded some answer to the vexed question of rights of trade and settlement in America. The New World came, in this way, to be incorporated during the course of the seventeenth century into the legalistic framework devised for a Europe of sovereign states.

By the middle of the seventeenth century, then, the Indies were something more than a field for missionary enterprise, and a juridical and territorial appanage of the Crowns of Castile and Portugal. Increasingly over the past century they had been integrated into the political, diplomatic and economic systems of Early Modern Europe, just as they had also been gradually integrated into its system of thought. 'There is only one world', wrote the Inca Garcilaso, 'and although we speak of the Old World and the New, this is because the latter was lately discovered by us, and not because there are two.'[3]

This world was to be pre-eminently a European world, in which overseas possessions came to be seen as essential adjuncts of Europe, enhancing the military and economic power of its rival nation-states. The conquest of America represented a decisive stage in this process, giving Europe new confidence in its own capacities, new territories and sources of wealth, and a new and deeper awareness of the complex interrelationship between treasure, population and trade, as the basis of national power. Occasionally, as they contemplated the conquest and its aftermath, Europeans had their moments of doubt. Ronsard, nostalgic for the primaeval innocence of the Golden Age, wondered whether the Indians of Brazil might not one day have cause to regret the benefits of civilization brought by Villegaignon.[4] Montaigne, after reading Gómara's *History*, suddenly

[1] Höffner, *Christentum und Menschenwürde*, p. 235. [2] *Ibid.* p. 253.
[3] *Royal Commentaries*, i, 9
[4] Elizabeth Armstrong, *Ronsard and the Age of Gold* (Cambridge, 1968), pp. 27–8.

grasped the full horror of the conquest: 'So many goodly citties ransacked and razed; so many nations destroyed and made desolate; so infinite millions of harmelesse people of all sexes, states and ages, massacred, ravaged and put to the sword; and the richest, the fairest and the best part of the world topsiturvied, ruined and defaced for the traffick of Pearles and Pepper . . .'[1] Even La Popelinière, the advocate of colonization, displayed a revealing moment of hesitation when he observed how the Europeans of his own century had risked their lives, their riches, their honour and their conscience 'to trouble the ease of those who, as our brethren in this great house of the world, asked only to live the rest of their days in peace and contentment'.[2]

But the doubts and the guilt were held in check by the firm conviction of the superior merits of Christianity and civility. A Europe newly convinced of the innate sinfulness of man, and increasingly conscious of the need for a powerful state organization to restrain the forces of disorder, had little inclination to idealize the virtues of primitive societies. Little was left of the America of the Golden Age once the generation of the humanists had passed away. The Europe of the Counter-Reformation and the Thirty Years War was more inclined to dwell on the virtues of the organized societies of the Aztecs and the Incas. But the praise was infrequent, and often grudging. Acosta believed that in some respects the American empires had the advantage 'over many of our republics'.[3] Botero, who had read his Acosta, admired the achievements of Mexico and Peru, but at those points where they most closely resembled the achievements of Europe.[4]

The New World, it seemed, had been accepted and absorbed— absorbed into a Europe whose triumphs over the Islamic peoples of the East and the heathen peoples of the West had made it arrogantly self-assured. In material terms it had gained much from America; in spiritual and intellectual terms it had gained less. But even here there had been an enrichment of experience which did

[1] 'Des Coches', in *The Essayes of Michael Lord of Montaigne*, trans. by John Florio (1603) (London, 1928), iii, 144.
[2] *Les Trois Mondes*, p. 38.   [3] *Historia Natural y Moral*, p. 280.
[4] Rosario Romeo, *Le Scoperte Americane*, pp. 103 ff. See Federico Chabod, 'Giovanni Botero', *Scritti sul Rinascimento* (Turin, 1967), pp. 417–24 for Botero's use of Acosta.

not leave Europe as it found it. Between 1492 and 1650 Europeans had discovered something about the world around them, and a good deal more about themselves. Ironically, the impact of this discovery was blunted by the very extent and completeness of their successes overseas. These successes ministered to the vanity of Europe, or at least of the official Europe of sovereign nation-states, which placed a high premium on the virtues of political and social stability, and conformity. Such a Europe was unlikely to show itself unduly receptive to new impressions and experiences.

But there existed another, and dissident, Europe which had not yet exhausted the possibilities of the New World so unexpectedly revealed on the far shores of the Atlantic. This was a Europe which rated freedom above authority, equality above hierarchy, and inquiry above acceptance. This other Europe would continue to turn, as it had turned in the days of the humanists, to America as a source of inspiration and hope. For if America nurtured Europe's ambitions, it also kept its dreams alive. And perhaps dreams were always more important than realities in the relationship of the Old World and the New.

SELECT BIBLIOGRAPHY

A bibliography of works covering different aspects of the impact of America on Europe in the sixteenth and early seventeenth centuries is all too likely to turn into a general bibliography of a century and a half of European history. I have therefore confined myself to a rigorously personal selection of those works which I found especially helpful in preparing this book, in the editions (or, in some cases, the translations) which I employed. Those books which, either in themselves or through their references, provide a useful introduction to the general theme of the relationship between the Old World and the New in the period under discussion, are starred with an asterisk.[1]

PRIMARY SOURCES[2]

Acosta, José de, *De Procuranda Indorum Salute*, Spanish trans. by Francisco Mateos (Madrid, 1952).

Historia Natural y Moral de las Indias, ed. Edmundo O'Gorman (2nd, revised, ed., FC, Mexico, 1962).

Arber, Edward (ed.), *The First Three English Books on America* (Birmingham, 1885).

The Works of Francis Bacon, ed. J. Spedding (14 vols., London, 1857–74).

Barlow, Roger, *A Brief Summe of Geographie*, ed. E. G. R. Taylor (HS, 2nd series, no. 69, London, 1932).

Benzoni, Girolamo, *La Historia del Mondo Nuovo* (Venice, 1565). Facsimile edition, Graz, 1962. English trans, by W. H. Smyth, *History of the New World* (HS, 1st series, vol. 21, London, 1857).

Bodin, Jean, *Method for the Easy Comprehension of History*, trans. Beatrice Reynolds (New York, 1945).

La Response de Jean Bodin a M. de Malestroit, 1568, ed. Henri Hauser (Paris, 1932).

---

[1] Abbreviations: BAE=Biblioteca de Autores Españoles; FC=Fondo de Cultura Económica; HS=Hakluyt Society.

[2] For bibliographical details of early Americana, see especially Henry Harrisse, *Bibliotheca Americana vetustissima. A Description of Works Relating to America, 1492–1551* (New York, 1866; reprinted, 3 vols., Madrid, 1958).

Select bibliography

The Six Bookes of a Commonweale, trans. Richard Knolles (1606). Facsimile, ed. by Kenneth D. McRae (Cambridge, Mass., 1962).

Boemus, Johannes, *The Manners, Laws and Customs of All Nations*, trans. Aston (London, 1611). Includes selections from Jean de Léry.

Colón, Hernando, *Vida del Almirante Cristóbal Colón* (FC, Mexico, 1947).

Columbus, Christopher, *The Journal of Christopher Columbus*, trans. Cecil Jane, ed. L. A. Vigneras (London, 1960).

Select Documents Illustrating the Four Voyages of Columbus, ed. Cecil Jane (HS, 2nd series, nos. 65 and 70, London, 1930–2).

Cortés, Hernán, *Cartas y Documentos*, ed. Mario Hernández Sánchez-Barba (Mexico, 1963).

De Pauw, Cornelius, *Recherches Philosophiques sur les Américains* (vols. 1–3 of *Œuvres Philosophiques*, Paris, 1794).

Eden, Richard, see Arber, *The First Three English Books*.

Enríquez de Guzmán, Alonso, *Libro de la Vida y Costumbres de Don Alonso Enríquez de Guzmán*, ed. Hayward Keniston (BAE, vol. 126, Madrid, 1960).

Ercilla, Alonso de, *La Araucana* (Clásicos de Chile, vol. 2, Santiago de Chile, 1956).

Esteve Barba, Francisco (ed.), *Crónicas Peruanas de Interés Indígena* (BAE, vol. 209, Madrid, 1968).

Fernández de Oviedo, Gonzalo, *Historia General y Natural de las Indias*, (BAE, vols. 117–21, Madrid, 1959).

Sumario de la Natural Historia de las Indias (FC, Mexico, 1950).

García, Gregorio, *Origen de los Indios del Nuevo Mundo y Indias Occidentales* (Valencia, 1607).

Garcilaso de la Vega, el Inca, *Royal Commentaries of the Incas*, trans. H. V. Livermore (2 vols., Austin, Texas, 1966).

The Voyages and Colonising Enterprises of Sir Humphrey Gilbert, ed. D. B. Quinn (HS, 2nd series, nos. 83–4, London, 1940).

Gómara, see López de Gómara.

Hakluyt, Richard, *The Original Writings and Correspondence of the Two Richard Hakluyts*, ed. E. G. R. Taylor (HS, 2nd series, nos. 76–7, London, 1935).

Jiménez de la Espada, Marcos, *Relaciones Geográficas de Indias. Perú* (Madrid, 1881–97, reprinted BAE vols. 183–5, Madrid, 1965).

Julien, C. A., Herval, R., Beauchesne, T., ed. *Les Français en Amérique pendant la première moitié du XVIe siècle* (Paris, 1946). Includes Verrazano's voyage.

La Popelinière, Henri de, *Les Trois Mondes* (Paris, 1582).

Select bibliography

Las Casas, Bartolomé de, *Apologética Historia Sumaria*, ed. Edmundo O'Gorman (2 vols., Mexico, 1967).

Historia de las Indias, ed. A. Millares Carlo and L. Hanke (3 vols., FC, Mexico, 1951).

Tratados (2 vols., FC, Mexico, 1965). Includes the *Brevísima Relación de la Destruición de las Indias.*

Léry, Jean de, *Histoire d'un Voyage fait en la Terre du Bresil, autrement dite Amérique* (La Rochelle, 1578).

Lescarbot, Marc, *The History of New France* (3 vols., original text with English trans., Toronto, 1907–14).

López de Gómara, Francisco, *Primera Parte de la Historia General de las Indias* (BAE, vol. 22, Madrid, 1852).

López de Velasco, Juan, *Geografía y Descripción Universal de las Indias*, ed. Justo Zaragoza (Madrid, 1894).

Mártir de Anglería, Pedro, *Décadas del Nuevo Mundo*, Spanish trans. by Joaquín Torres Asensio (Buenos Aires, 1944).

Epistolario, ed. José López de Toro (Documentos Inéditos para la Historia de España, vols. ix–xii, Madrid, 1953–7).

Mercado, Tomás de, *Summa de Tratos y Contratos* (Seville, 1571).

Monardes, Nicolás, *Joyfull Newes out of the Newe Founde Worlde*, trans. John Frampton (1577), ed. Stephen Gaselee (2 vols., London 1925).

Montaigne, Michel de, *Essais* (Pléiade, Paris, 1950). 'Des Cannibales'; 'Des Coches'.

Montalboddo, Francanzano de, *Paesi Novamente Retrovati* (Venice, 1507).

Otte, Enrique (ed.), 'Cartas Privadas de Puebla del Siglo XVI', *Jahrbuch für Geschichte von Staat, Wirtschaft und Gesellschaft Lateinamerikas*, iii (1966), 10–87.

Palacios Rubios, Juan López de, *De las Islas del Mar Océano*, ed. S. Zavala and A. Millares Carlo (FC, Mexico, 1954).

Pellicer de Ossau, José, *Comercio Impedido* (Madrid, 1640). (Catalogued in British Museum under *Comercio* but not under Pellicer.)

Pérez de Oliva, Hernán, *Historia de la Invención de las Yndias*, ed. José Juan Arrom (Bogotá, 1965).

Las Obras (Córdoba, 1586).

Quinn, D. B. (ed.), *The Roanoke Voyages, 1584–90* (HS, 2nd series, nos. 104–5, London, 1955).

Raleigh, Sir Walter, *The Discoverie of the Large, Rich and Bewtiful Empyre of Guiana* (1596). Facsimile ed., Leeds, 1967.

Ramusio, Giovanni Battista, *Terzo Volume delle Navigationi et Viaggi*

Select bibliography

(Venice, 1556). *See also* George B. Parks, *The Contents and Sources of Ramusio's Navigationi* (New York Public Library, 1955).

Raynal (Reynal), Guillaume, *A Philosophical and Political History of the Settlements and Trade of the Europeans in the East and West Indies*, trans. J. Justamond (4 vols., Dublin, 1776).

Sahagún, Bernardino de, *Historia General de las Cosas de Nueva España*, ed. Miguel Acosta Saignes (3 vols., Mexico, 1946).

General History of the Things of New Spain; Florentine Codex, trans. and ed. A. J. O. Anderson and C. E. Dibble (13 parts, Santa Fe, from 1950).

Sepúlveda, Juan Ginés de, *Demócrates Segundo*, ed. Angel Losada (Madrid, 1951).

Epistolario, ed. Angel Losada (Madrid, 1966).

Smith, Adam, *The Wealth of Nations*, ed. Edwin Cannan (London, 1904, reprinted 2 vols., University Paperbacks, London, 1961).

Staden, Hans, *The True History of His Captivity*, ed. M. Letts (London, 1928).

Stock, L. F. (ed.), *Proceedings and Debates of the British Parliaments Respecting North America*, vol. i (1542–1688) (Washington, 1924).

Suárez de Figueroa, Cristóbal, *El Passagero* (1617, ed. Sociedad de Bibliófilos Españoles, vol. 38, Madrid, 1914).

Thevet, André, *Les Singularitez de la France Antarctique* (Antwerp, 1558).

Tovar, Juan de, *Historia de la Venida de los Yndios a poblar a Mexico de las partes remotas de Occidente* (manuscript in John Carter Brown Library, Providence, Rhode Island).

Vargas Machuca, Bernardo de, *Milicia y Descripción de las Indias* (Madrid, 1599).

Vedia, Enrique de (ed.), *Historiadores Primitivos de Indias* (BAE, vols. 22 and 26, Madrid, 1852–3).

Veitia Linage, Joseph de, *Norte de la Contratación de las Indias Occidentales* (1672, reprinted Buenos Aires, 1945).

Vitoria, Francisco de, *Obras*, ed. Teófilo Urdánoz (Biblioteca de Autores Cristianos, vol. 198, Madrid, 1960).

Relectio de Indis, ed. L. Pereña and J. M. Pérez Prendes (Corpus Hispanorum de Pace, vol. v, Madrid, 1967).

Zorita, Alonso de, *Breve y Sumaria Relación de los Señores de la Nueva España* (*The Lords of New Spain*, trans. Benjamin Keen, Rutgers 1963, London, 1965).

Select bibliography

SECONDARY AUTHORITIES

Allen, Don Cameron, *The Legend of Noah* (Illinois Studies in Language and Literature, vol. xxxiii, nos. 3–4, Urbana, 1949).

Andrews, K. R., *Elizabethan Privateering* (Cambridge, 1964).

Drake's Voyages (London, 1967).

Armstrong, Elizabeth, *Ronsard and the Age of Gold* (Cambridge, 1968).

Arnoldsson, Sverker, *La Leyenda Negra* (Göteborg, 1960).

*Atkinson, Geoffroy, *Les Nouveaux Horizons de la Renaissance Française* (Paris, 1935).

Bataillon, Marcel, *Etudes sur Bartolomé de las Casas* (Paris, 1965).

Baudet, Henri, *Paradise on Earth* (New Haven–London, 1965).

Bernheimer, Richard, *Wild Men in the Middle Ages* (Cambridge, Mass., 1952).

Boxer, C. R., *The Portuguese Seaborne Empire, 1415–1825* (London, 1969).

Boyd-Bowman, Peter, *Indice Geobiográfico de Cuarenta Mil Pobladores Españoles de América en el Siglo XVI*, vol. i. (Bogotá, 1964).

Callot, Emile, *La Renaissance des Sciences de la Vie au XVIe Siècle* (Paris, 1951).

The Cambridge Economic History of Europe, vol. iv, ed. E. E. Rich and C. H. Wilson (Cambridge, 1967).

Carbia, Rómulo D., *Historia de la Leyenda Negra Hispanoamericana*. (Madrid, 1944).

La Crónica Oficial de las Indias Occidentales (Buenos Aires, 1940).

Carvalho, Joaquim de, *Estudos sobre a Cultura Portuguesa do Século XVI*, vol. i (Coimbra, 1947).

Cawley, R. R., *Unpathed Waters* (Princeton, 1940).

Cermentati, Mario, 'Ulisse Aldrovandi e l'America', *Annali di Botanica*, iv (Rome, 1906), 313–66.

Chardon, Carlos E., *Los Naturalistas en la América Latina*, vol. i (Ciudad Trujillo, 1949).

Chaunu, Huguette and Pierre, *Séville et l'Atlantique, 1504–1650* (8 vols., Paris, 1955–9).

Chaunu, Pierre, *L'Amérique et les Amériques* (Paris, 1964).

'Séville et la "Belgique", 1555–1648', *Revue du Nord*, xlii (1960), 259–92.

*Chinard, Gilbert, *L'Exotisme Américain dans la Littérature Française au XVIe Siècle* (Paris, 1911).

*Chinard, Gilbert, *L'Amérique et le Rêve Exotique dans la Littérature Française au XVIIe et au XVIIIe Siècle* (Paris, 1913).

Select bibliography

Cioranescu, Alejandro, *Colón, Humanista* (Madrid, 1967).

*Crone, G. R., *The Discovery of America* (London, 1969).

Dacos, Nicole, 'Présents Américains à la Renaissance. L'Assimilation de l'Exotisme', *Gazette des Beaux-Arts*, VIe période, vol. lxxiii (1969), 57–64.

Dainville, François de, *La Géographie des Humanistes* (Paris, 1940).

Davis, David Brion, *The Problem of Slavery in Western Culture* (Ithaca, 1966).

La Découverte de L'Amérique (Dixième Stage International d'Etudes Humanistes, Tours, 1966) (Paris, 1968).

Domínguez Ortiz, Antonio, *Orto y Ocaso de Sevilla* (Seville, 1946).
  Política y Hacienda de Felipe IV (Madrid, 1960).

Echeverria, Durand, *Mirage in the West* (Princeton, 1957, repr. 1968).

Esteve Barba, Francisco, *Historiografía Indiana* (Madrid, 1964).

Fernández Alvarez, Manuel, *Política Mundial de Carlos V y Felipe II* (Madrid, 1966).

Gentil Da Silva, José, *En Espagne* (Paris, 1965).

Gerbi, Antonello, *La Disputa del Nuovo Mondo* (Milan, 1955. Spanish trans., *La Disputa del Nuevo Mundo*, FC, Mexico, 1960).

Glacken, Clarence J., *Traces on the Rhodian Shore. Nature and Culture in Western Thought from Ancient Times to the End of the Eighteenth Century* (Berkeley, 1967).

Guerra, Francisco, *Nicolás Bautista Monardes. Su Vida y su Obra* (Mexico, 1961).

*Hale, John, 'A World Elsewhere', *The Age of the Renaissance*, ed. Denys Hay (London, 1967), pp. 317–43.

Hamilton, Earl J., *American Treasure and the Price Revolution in Spain, 1501–1650* (Cambridge, Mass., 1934).
  'American Treasure and the Rise of Capitalism', *Economica*, ix (1929), 338–57.

Hanke, Lewis, *Aristotle and the American Indians* (London, 1959).
  Estudios sobre Fray Bartolomé de las Casas y sobre la Lucha por la Justicia en la Conquista Española de América (Caracas, 1968).
  The Spanish Struggle for Justice in the Conquest of America (Philadelphia, 1949).

Hay, Denys, *Europe—the Emergence of an Idea* (Edinburgh, 1957).

*Hodgen, Margaret T., *Early Anthropology in the Sixteenth and Seventeenth Centuries* (Philadelphia, 1964).

Höffner, Joseph, *Christentum und Menschenwürde. Das Anliegen der Spanischen Kolonialethik im Goldenen Zeitalter* (Trier, 1947).

Select bibliography

Hulton, Paul, and Quinn, D. B., *The American Drawings of John White, 1577–1590* (2 vols., London, 1964).

Humboldt, Alexander Von, *Cosmos* (2 vols., London, 1845–8).

Hussey, R. D., 'America in European Diplomacy, 1597–1604', *Revista de Historia de América*, no. 41 (1956), 1–30.

*Jones, Howard Mumford, *O Strange New World* (New York, 1964).

Jordan, Winthrop D., *White Over Black* (Chapel Hill, 1968).

Julien, C. A., *Les Débuts de l'Expansion et de la Colonisation Française* (Paris, 1947).

Larsen, Erik, *Frans Post* (Amsterdam–Rio de Janeiro, 1962).

Lewis, Archibald R., and McGann, Thomas F. (ed.), *The New World Looks at its History* (Austin, Texas, 1963).

Lohmann Villena, Guillermo, *Les Espinosa* (Paris, 1968).

Lynch, John, *Spain under the Habsburgs* (2 vols., Oxford, 1964–9).

Maravall, José Antonio, *Antiguos y Modernos* (Madrid, 1966), pp. 429–53 ('La Circunstancia del Descubrimiento de América').

Mateos, Francisco, 'Ecos de América en Trento', *Revista de Indias*, 22 (1945), 559–605.

*Menéndez-Pidal, Gonzalo, *Imagen del Mundo Hacia 1570* (Madrid, 1944).

Mollat, Michel, and Adam, Paul (ed.), *Les Aspects Internationaux de la Découverte Océanique aux XVe et XVIe Siècles* (Actes du Cinquième Colloque International d'Histoire Maritime) (Paris, 1966).

Morínigo, Marcos A., *América en el Teatro de Lope de Vega* (Buenos Aires, 1946).

Morison, Samuel Eliot, *Admiral of the Ocean Sea. A Life of Christopher Columbus* (2 vols., Boston, 1942).

*Myres, J. L., 'The Influence of Anthropology on the Course of Political Science', *University of California Publications in History*, iv, no. 1 (1916), 1–81.

Newton, A. P., *The European Nations in the West Indies, 1493–1688* (London, 1933, repr. 1966).

*O'Gorman, Edmundo, *The Invention of America* (Bloomington, 1961).

Olschki, Leonardo, *Storia Letteraria delle Scoperte Geografiche* (Florence, 1937).

'What Columbus Saw on Landing in the West Indies', *Proceedings of the American Philosophical Society*, 84 (1941), 633–59.

Palm, Erwin Walter, *Los Monumentos Arquitectónicos de la Española*, vol. i (Ciudad Trujillo, 1955).

'Tenochtitlan y la Ciudad Ideal de Dürer', *Journal de la Société des Américanistes*, nouvelle série, xl (Paris, 1951), 59–66.

Select bibliography

Papi, Fulvio, *Antropologia e Civiltà Nel Pensiero Di Giordano Bruno* (Florence, 1968).

Parker, John (ed.), *Merchants and Scholars* (Minneapolis, 1965).

Parks, G. B., *Richard Hakluyt and the English Voyages* (New York, 1928).

Parry, J. H., *The Age of Reconnaissance* (London, 1963).

The Spanish Seaborne Empire (London, 1966).

The Spanish Theory of Empire in the Sixteenth Century (Cambridge, 1940).

Pedro, Valentín de, *América en las Letras Españolas del Siglo de Oro* (Buenos Aires, 1954).

*Penrose, Boies, *Travel and Discovery in the Renaissance, 1420–1620* (Cambridge, Mass., 1960).

Phelan, John Leddy, *The Millenial Kingdom of the Franciscans in the New World* (Berkeley, 1956).

Pike, Ruth, *Enterprise and Adventure. The Genoese in Seville and the Opening of the New World* (Ithaca, 1966).

Pulido Rubio, José, *El Piloto Mayor de la Casa de la Contratación de Sevilla* (Seville, 1950).

*Quinn, D. B., 'Exploration and the Expansion of Europe', *Rapports* of the XII International Congress of Historical Sciences, i (Vienna, 1965), 45–59.

Rey Pastor, Julio, *La Ciencia y la Técnica en el Descubrimiento de América* (3rd ed., Colección Austral, Buenos Aires, 1951).

Robertson, H. M., *Aspects of the Rise of Economic Individualism* (Cambridge, 1935).

*Romeo, Rosario, *Le Scoperte Americane nella Coscienza Italiana del Cinquecento* (Milan–Naples, 1954).

Rosen, Edward, 'Copernicus and the Discovery of America', *Hispanic American Historical Review*, xxiii (1943), 367–71.

*Rowe, John H., 'Ethnography and Ethnology in the Sixteenth Century', *The Kroeber Anthropological Society Papers*, no. 30 (1964), 1–19.

Rowse, A. L., *The Elizabethans and America* (London, 1959).

Salas, Alberto M., *Tres Cronistas de Indias. Pedro Mártir, Oviedo, Las Casas* (FC, Mexico, 1959).

Sanford, Charles L., *The Quest for Paradise. Europe and the American Moral Imagination* (Urbana, 1961).

*Scammell, G. V., 'The New Worlds and Europe in the Sixteenth Century', *The Historical Journal*, xii (1969), 389–412.

Scott, J. B., *The Spanish Origin of International Law* (Oxford, 1934).

Schafer, Edward H., *The Vermilion Bird* (Berkeley, 1967).

Select bibliography

Šimeček, Zdeněk, 'L'Amérique au 16e siècle à la lumière des nouvelles du service de renseignements de la famille des Rožmberk', *Historica*, xi (Prague, 1965), 53–93.

Spooner, Frank C., *L'Economie Mondiale et les Frappes Monétaires en France, 1493–1680* (Paris, 1956).

Tazbir, Janusz, 'La conquête de l'Amérique à la lumière de l'opinion polonaise', *Acta Poloniae Historica*, xvii (1968), 5–22.

Verlinden, Charles, and Pérez-Embid, Florentino, *Cristóbal Colón y el Descubrimiento de América* (Madrid, 1967).

Vilar, Pierre, *Crecimiento y Desarollo* (Barcelona, 1964).

Vivanti, C., 'Alle origini dell' idea di civiltà: le scoperte geografiche e gli scritti di Henri de la Popelinière', *Rivista Storica Italiana*, lxxiv (1962), 225–49.

Washburn, W. E., 'The Meaning of "Discovery" in the Fifteenth and Sixteenth Centuries', *American Historical Review*, lxviii (1962), 1–21.

Webb, Walter Prescott, *The Great Frontier* (London, 1953).

Winch, Peter, 'Understanding a Primitive Society', *Religion and Understanding*, ed. D. Z. Phillips (Oxford, 1967).

Essays Honoring Lawrence C. Wroth (Portland, Maine, 1951).

Zavala, Silvio, *La Filosofía Política en la Conquista de América* (Mexico, 1947).

Las Instituciones Jurídicas en la Conquista de América (Madrid, 1935).

La 'Utopia' de Tomás Moro en la Nueva España y Otros Ensayos (Mexico, 1937).

Sir Thomas More in New Spain (Diamante III, The Hispanic and Luso-Brazilian Councils, London, 1955).

INDEX

absolutism, 79–83
Académie Française, 2, 4
Acosta, José de, 30–1, 34–5, 39, 41, 48–52, 81, 103
Aldrete, Bernardo, 36
Aldrovandi, Ulisse, 38
America, discovery of, 8–12; literature on, 12–13; descriptions of, 18–23; plants and wildlife, 14, 19, 21–2, 31, 37–8; see also Indians
anthropology, see ethnology
architecture, 45
Aristotle, 30, 39, 42, 44, 47–8
art, European, and America, 21–3, 32, 50, 65; native, 32, 45
artists, 21–3, 32, 50, 95
Atkinson, Geoffrey, 5
Azpilcueta Navarro, Martín de, 63
Aztecs, see Mexico

Bacon, Sir Francis, 11, 51, 83, 87
Baltic trade, 70
bankers, 86, 90, 99
barbarism, 26, 32, 42, 44–53, 81
Barlowe, Arthur, 19
Benzoni, Girolamo, 11, 95
Berruguete, Alonso, 21
Betanzos, Juan de, 18
Bible, 25, 29–30, 46–7, 49–50
Black Legend, 95–6
Bodin, Jean, 14, 49, 53, 62, 83
botany, 31, 37–8
Botero, Giovanni, 103
Braudel, Fernand, 67, 78, 79
Brazil, depictions of, 19, 22–3; natives of, 43, 51, 53, 102; European powers and, 91, 98–100
Britons, Ancient, 50
Bry, Théodore de, 23, 95
Buonamico, Lazzaro, 9
Buonincontri, Lorenzo, 40

Calvin, 43, 57
cannibalism, 27, 34

capitalism, 55–9, 62, 66–7
Carew, Sir Peter, 92
Castile, 35, 37; America and economy of, 60, 63–7, 73–7, 96–7; and possession of Indies, 80–1, 82, 94, 100–2; absolutism in, 81–2; see also Spain
Castro, Alfonso de, 102
Catalans, 96, 100
Cateau-Cambrésis, peace of, 86, 92, 100–1
Chanca, Dr, 42
Charles V, 14, 84–7, 90, 91
Chaunu, Pierre, 56–7, 68–9, 71, 86, 88–9
Chinard, Gabriel, 5
Chinese, 16–17, 21, 31, 49, 55
Christianity, 30–1, 41–52, 103; spread of, 11, 12, 25, 31, 33–4, 80–1, 94; native fitness for, 43, 45; see also church; religious orders
chroniclers, Spanish, 5–6, 19, 21–2; of the Indies, 38, 96
church, 79–81, 100, 101; see also Christianity
Cicero, 48
civilization, 26, 41, 44–53, 94, 102–3
classical tradition, 15–16, 23, 24–6, 30, 32, 39–52, 94; see also Golden Age
climate, 49
Coligny, Admiral, 91, 92, 98
Colón, Hernando, 10
colonization, 70–1, 74, 76–8, 82, 83–4, 92–3
colour, 22, 43–4
Columbus, Christopher, 8–12, 24–5, 42, 58
Córdoba, 73–4, 75
Cortés, Hernán, 12, 19, 30, 46, 84–5
cosmography, see geography
Counter Reformation, 80, 103
cultural diversity, 48–9

Danube peasant, 26
De Pauw, Cornelius, 1

115

Index

Díaz, Bernal, 13, 20
discovery, reactions to, 8–15
Downs, battle of the, 100
Drake, Sir Francis, 93, 94
Duplessis-Mornay, Philippe, 92, 98
Durán, Fray Diego, 33, 35
Dürer, Albrecht, 32
Dutch, 22–3, 95, 97–100

Eden, garden of, 24–5
Eden, Richard, 91
emigration, 75–7, 83–4
empire, westward movement of, 73, 94; of
    Charles V, 84–7; Spanish, 87–94, 96–7,
    100; Portuguese, 98–100; see also
    imperialism
England, 41, 66, 84; interest in New
    World, 12, 91–2, 94, 95, 100, 101
Enríquez de Guzmán, Alonso, 20
Ercilla, Alonso de, 12
Espinosa family, 67, 75
ethnology, 6, 32, 33, 35, 48

Ferdinand the Catholic, 11, 80
Fernández de Oviedo, Gonzalo, 11, 35,
    40; on wonders of America, 21, 31;
    methods of, 32, 37, 41; on Indians, 34,
    43; on Spain and the Indies, 59, 63, 78,
    88
Florida, 50, 92, 94, 95
Frampton, John, 38
France, 83, 84, 99; literature on America,
    5, 12, 95; designs on America, 91–2,
    100–1
Francis I, 100
friars, see religious orders
Frontier, Great, 58, 73, 77, 83

García, Gregorio, 29–30
Garcilaso de la Vega, el Inca, 36, 51, 64,
    102
Geneva, 95
Genoese, 74, 75, 86, 96, 99
geography, 11, 12, 14, 15, 38–41, 49
Gerbi, Antonello, 5
Germany, 84, 86, 89–90
Gilbert, Sir Humphrey, 82, 94
gold, 11, 60–1, 65, 71–2, 96, 97
Golden Age, 21, 24–5, 42, 52, 102, 103;
    see also classical tradition
Gómara, see López de Gómara
González de Cellorigo, Martín, 96
Granada, 81, 83

Grotius, 102
Guevara, Antonio de, 26
Guiana, 22
Guicciardini, Francesco, 9, 28–9

Hakluyt, Richard, 83, 90
Hamilton, Earl J., 55–6, 59, 64, 66
Hayes, Edward, 94
Hawkins, Sir John, 93
Hernández, Dr Francisco, 38
Herrera, Antonio de, 38
Heyn, Piet, 98
Hispaniola, 20, 22, 37, 42, 78
historiography, 34–5, 38–9, 50–2; of
    America's impact on Europe, 3–4, 6–7,
    54–9
Hodgen, Margaret, 6
humanists, 12, 18, 25–7, 103, 104; see also
    Renaissance
Humboldt, Alexander von, 3, 5, 18, 19

imperialism, 79–86, 88–9, 94, 96
Incas, see Peru
Indians, nakedness, 8, 25; religion, 9, 33–
    4, 43, 45, see also Christianity; language,
    18–19, 34, 36, 49; descriptions of, 20,
    22–3, 26; nature of, 21, 24, 39–53;
    origins and history, 30, 38–9, 41, 49–
    50; political and social organization,
    33, 45, 48–9, 103; Spanish treatment of,
    44, 88, 95–6, 103; population decline,
    70, 95; see also Mexico; Peru
Indies, chronicler of, 38, 96
industry, 54–6, 62, 67, 68, 96
innocence, 5, 25–6, 42, 46
Ireland, 34, 82
Islam, 14, 17, 60, 87–8, 103
Italy, 12, 66, 82, 87, 90, 93

John Maurice, Prince of Nassau, 22

language, 17, 18, 34, 36, 49
La Popelinière, Henri de, 83, 103
Las Casas, Bartolomé de, 21, 31, 40, 41,
    95–6; and Indians, 33, 34, 45, 48–9
Le Roy, Louis, 9
Léry, Jean de, 19, 22, 43, 53
Lescarbot, Marc, 76
Lipsius, Justus, 63
Lope de Vega Carpio, Félix, 11
López de Gómara, Francisco de, 13, 52,
    78, 81, 88, 102; on significance of
    discovery, 10; on prices, 62
López de Velasco, Juan, 38

116

Index

Luther, Martin, 57–8

Madrid, 65, 83, 101
Mandeville, Sir John, 24
Mantegna, Andrea, 21
Mantuan Succession, war of the, 98
Martyr, Peter, 8–9, 26, 88, 91, 95
Marx, Karl, 55
Mary I, Tudor, 91
Medina del Campo, 65
Mela, Pomponius, 14
Mercado, Fray Tomás de, 21, 44, 74, 75
merchants, 12, 65, 90, 91, 99; of Seville, 21, 71, 74–5, 99; and profits, 61, 62, 67–8
mercury, 70
Mexico, 20, 27, 70–1, 76, 84; art and civilization, 19, 32, 45, 46, 48, 49, 103; history, 34–5, 41
Milan, 82, 90
mines, 61, 70–2, 74, 85, 86, 90
missionaries, *see* religious orders
Monardes, Nicolás, 37–8
Montaigne, Michel de, 13, 102
Montalboddo, Francanzano, 9
Montezuma, 32, 84
Moors, 24, 83
Morales, Ambrosio de, 36
More, Sir Thomas, 26
Münster, treaty of, 101
Murad III, 88
myth, the American, 5, 26–7, 94, 103

Negroes, 24, 44
Netherlands, 86; *see also* Dutch
Noah, 49
Nunes, Pedro, 39

O'Gorman, Edmundo, 5
Olivares, conde duque de, 96, 98–100
Otto of Freising, 94
Ovando, Juan de, 36–7, 38
Oxenham, Henry, 93

Panama, isthmus of, 92–3
papal bulls, 43, 80
papal donation, 80–1, 100, 101
Pasquier, Etienne, 8, 51
Paul III, 43
Pellicer de Ossau, José, 74, 99
Pérez de Oliva, Hernán, 15, 26, 60, 73–4, 75, 94
Peru, 62, 70–1, 83, 85; pre-conquest, 18,

48, 49, 51, 103
Philip II, 38, 82, 87, 88, 90, 93
Philip III, 44, 89, 97
philology, 36
Pliny, 32
Poland, 13
Ponet, John, 92
population, 66, 70, 72, 75, 77
Portugal, 8, 82, 97–100
Post, Frans, 22–3
privateers, 86, 91
progress, 52–3
Protestantism, 43, 55–8, 93, 94–5
Ptolemy, 14, 40

questionnaires, 33–7
Quiroga, Vasco de, 27

race, 4, 24, 43–4
Raleigh, Sir Walter, 22
Ramusio, Giovanni Battista, 9, 11, 37
rationality, 43–5, 48–9
Raynal, Abbé, 1–2, 4, 54–5, 58
relativism, 29
religious orders, 25–7, 28, 33–4, 43, 80, 81; *see also* Christianity
Renaissance, 3, 14–15, 24, 41–2, 56, 57; *see also* humanists
Ribault, Jean, 92
Roanoke, 19, 22
Robertson, H. M., 57, 59
Ronsard, Pierre de, 102
Rudyard, Sir Benjamin, 90

Sahagún, Bernardino de, 35
St Teresa, 76–7
Salamanca, 40, 63
San Juan de Ulúa, 92, 94–5
Santo Tomás, Fray Domingo de, 34
Schafer, Edward, 16, 31
scholasticism, 47–8, 62, 81, 82, 85, 101
sea-power, 87, 93, 97, 100
Sepúlveda, Juan Ginés de, 44, 45, 85
Seville, 64–5, 74–5; trade, 68–71, 72, 85–7, 89–91, 97–100; *see also* merchants
silver, and trade with East, 56, 60–1, 66, 68, 70; and prices, 56, 61–4, 66, 68; remittances, 60–1, 64–6, 69–72, 77, 85–91, 97–100; fleets, 72, 91–3, 98, 100; and Spanish power, 90–1, 97–6
slavery, 4, 44, 98
Smith, Adam, 1, 54–5, 59

Index